Intermediate Level B

English Through Citizenship

Intermediate Level B

English
Through
Citizenship

Elaine Kirn
West Los Angeles College

Delta Systems Co., Inc.

First Edition

9 8 7 6 5 4 3 2

Published in The United States by Delta Systems Co., Inc.

ISBN 0-937354-44-9

Manufactured in the United States of America

Series Design and Production: Etcetera Graphics, Canoga Park, CA
Typesetting: Etcetera Graphics
Artist: Terry Wilson (Etcetera Graphics)

Acknowledgements

Thanks to the amnesty coordinators and instructors of the Los Angeles Community College District and surrounding schools for supporting this project and offering helpful suggestions, as well as to Victoria Richart of Los Angeles Mission College and the Los Angeles and Orange County curriculum committee for the creation of complete course outlines and guidelines. Special appreciation goes to Jon Hendershot of Los Angeles Southwest College and Jack Fujimoto of the LACCD for initiation of the project.

And as usual, thanks to a hard-working staff and freelancers:

John Dermody for research and initial drafts,
Pat Campbell for editing,
Terry Wilson for expressive artwork,
Suzette Mahr for typesetting,
Anthony Thorne-Booth for falling in love
        with the new computer,
Chuck Alessio for putting it all together,
and all of us for long, long workdays and evenings.

In advance, appreciation goes to Dick Patchin of Delta Systems and the sales staff for enthusiasm and being out there.

Contents

To The Student

Can you understand, speak, read, and write basic English? Do you want to learn about the customs, government, and history of your new country, state, and city in simplified English? Then the Intermediate Level of *English Through Citizenship* is the right level for you.

The information in this book will help you prepare for an Immigration and Naturalization (INS) examination for permanent residence or citizenship. You can study the information on your own. To check your answers, look at the Answer Key of the Intermediate Level Instructor's Manual.

You may also be using this book in a course in English as a Second Language at a public or private school that includes instruction in government and history. You can learn a great deal of vocabulary and information from *English Through Citizenship* before you try to read more difficult books in English.

If the language in the Intermediate Level of *English Through Citizenship* is too difficult for you, you can start your program of study at the Beginning Level.

To the Instructor

English Through Citizenship is a three-level program of simplified civics material for speakers of English as a Second Language.

The Intermediate Level of *English Through Citizenship* is designed for individuals who have some level of proficiency in understanding, speaking, reading, and writing the English language. A score between 191 and 216 on the CASAS (California Adult Student Assessment System) or a comparable score on another English language skills placement test indicates that an individual is likely to succeed with the materials at this level.

Students who score above 216 on the CASAS or who place into an advanced level on another placement test can profit from use of *English Through Citizenship* as preparation for more advanced texts, such as the three federal publications mentioned below.

English Through Citizenship is based on curriculum outlines developed by the Los Angeles Community College District (LACCD) and the Los Angeles County Community College Consortium for Amnesty (LACCCCA). These outlines have been approved by the California State Department of Education and the Immigration and Naturalization Service for implementation in classes funded by State Legislative Impact Assistance Grants (SLIAG) in accordance with the Immigration Reform and Control Act (IRCA).

The information in the program is derived largely from three texts issued by the federal government: *United States History 1600-1987*, *U.S. Government Structure*, and *Citizenship Education and Naturalization Information* (U.S. Department of Justice, Immigration and Naturalization Service, 1987).

Based on proven ESL methodology in language skills instruction (primarily listening, speaking, and reading), *English Through Citizenship* is designed for use by individuals applying for legalization status as permanent residents of the United States or for U.S. citizenship, as well as for general civics instruction in high schools and colleges.

The history, government, and citizenship material of the program is divided into twelve numbered units, each subdivided into several lettered modules. Because the material at this level is extensive, it is divided into two books: Intermediate Level A and Intermediate Level B. Each module consists of four pages of material, designed for one or more class periods of instruction with follow up (homework and/or review). The modules can be presented in book form or removed from the texts for use in any desired order.

For a complete listing of the material available at all three levels, see the Instructor's Manual.

Accompanying Materials

A pretest and posttest correspond to each four-page module. These can be ordered in perforated book form.

Accompanying each text is a detailed instructor's manual. Because it offers general and specific suggestions for presentation of the modules, it will not only streamline lesson planning for experienced teachers but can also serve as a training manual for new ones. It includes an Answer Key.

English Through Citizenship: A Question-and-Answer Game presents an opportunity in the ESL/Civics classroom for co-operative learning at the intermediate level. The questions and answers in this innovative game are based on the information in the federal textbooks published by the U.S. Department of Justice Immigration and Naturalization Service (1987).

For more information on accompanying materials, contact:

Delta Systems Co., Inc.
1400 Miller Parkway
McHenry, IL 60050–7030

Also to the Instructor

The Federal Government

Module 7A: Overview of U.S. Government

A   The American System of Government

The United States is a democratic republic (a representative democracy). The national government is a government of all the people and their representatives (elected officials). It is called the federal government because the nation is a federation, or association, of states.

The U.S. Constitution gave the federal government only limited powers, the powers stated in the Constitution. All other powers belong to the individual states.

The Founding Fathers established three branches of government: the legislative, the executive, and the judicial. Each branch has different functions and powers under the principle of separation of powers. There is also a system of checks and balances so that each branch has some control over the other two branches. This way, no one group can have too much power.

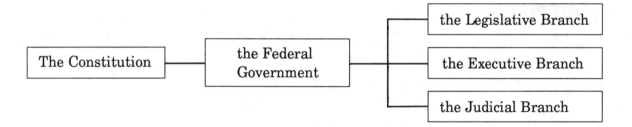

B   Match the words with their meanings. Write the letters on the lines.

1. ___ a democratic republic

2. ___ representatives and senators

3. ___ the Federal Government

4. ___ a federation d.

5. ___ limited powers

6. ___ the branches of government

7. ___ the separation of powers

8. ___ checks and balances

a. an association

b. having different functions

c. the legislative, the executive, and the judicial

d. only those powers stated in the Constitution

e. a government of the people (a representative democracy)

f. elected officials

g. the national government

h. a system of control of each branch over the other two

The Three Branches of Government

The legislative branch is called Congress. It consists of the Senate and the House of Representatives. It is the responsibility of Congress to propose and pass laws. In the system of checks and balances, Congress can refuse to approve Presidential appointments and can override a Presidential veto.

The executive branch consists of the President, the Vice President, the Cabinet and the thirteen Departments, and the independent agencies. It's the responsibility of the executive to enforce laws. The President has the power to veto (reject) any bill (law) of Congress. He appoints all Supreme Court Justices.

The judicial branch consists of the Supreme (highest) Court, eleven Circuit Courts of Appeals, and ninety-four District Courts. This branch explains and interprets laws and makes decisions in lawsuits. It has power over the other two branches because it can declare their laws and actions unconstitutional (against the principles of the Constitution).

 Answer these questions about the three branches of government.

	the Legislative	the Executive	the Judicial
1. What does it consist of?	the Senate		
	the House of		
	Representatives		
2. What are its responsibilities?			
3. What powers does it have under the system of checks and balances?			

E   Political Parties

The U.S. Constitution does not talk about political parties, but they began during George Washington's term of office. On one side were the Federalists. They wanted a strong federal government. On the other side, the Democratic-Republicans wanted to limit the power of the national government. Their leader was Thomas Jefferson, and their group later became the Democratic Party.

Some of the early political parties, such as the Federalists and the Whigs, no longer exist. Since 1854, the two major parties have been the Democrats and the Republicans. Smaller parties have lasted for only a short time. "Third parties" have won in local elections, but their candidates have never won a Presidential election.

Many people say that there is not much difference between the Republican and Democratic Parties. "Liberal" politicians usually favor reform (change) and progress. "Conservative" politicians usually oppose change. But both liberal and conservative members belong to the two major political parties, and their ideas often change with the times and the issues.

F   Write T for true and F for false. Correct the false sentences.

1. ___ Article 2 of the U.S. Constitution establishes political parties.

2. ___ During the time of George Washington, the Federalists supported a strong federal government, but the Democratic-Republicans wanted to limit government power.

3. ___ Thomas Jefferson was the leader of the Whigs, a third party in opposition to change.

4. ___ Since 1854, the two major political parties have been the Whigs and the Libertarians.

5. ___ Voters have elected some third-party candidates to local office but never to the Presidency.

6. ___ All Democrats are conservative and all Republicans are liberals.

7. ___ Liberal politicians usually support reform, and conservative candidates oppose it.

8. ___ Political parties, candidates, and their ideas have changed with the times and the issues.

G **Work in pairs. Each of you studies the information about a different one of the two major political parties. Summarize your information for your partner.**

1.  The Democratic Party is the oldest party in the United States. In 1828 Andrew Johnson became the first Democratic President. Since that time, the issues of the nation and the ideas of the party have changed. Both the major parties have liberal and conservative members, but in general people consider the Democrats today more liberal than the Republicans. Democrats often want the government to establish social programs for people in need, such as the poor, the unemployed, and the elderly. They usually say they believe in equal rights for women and minorities and they oppose nuclear weapons and too much military spending. The symbol of the Democratic Party (from political cartoons) is the donkey.

2.  The Republican Party, sometimes called the G.O.P. (the Grand Old Party) began in 1854 over the issue of slavery. Republicans opposed slavery. The first Republican candidate to become President was Abraham Lincoln. After the Civil War, Republicans got interested in farm, land, and business issues. In general, Republicans vote more conservatively than Democrats. They want government to support big business but not to control the lives of citizens. They often oppose government spending for social programs but support military spending. The party symbol is the elephant.

H **Which party is each sentence about? Write R for the Republican and D for the Democratic.**

1. ___ It is the oldest political party in the United States.

2. ___ It is sometimes called the G.O.P.

3. ___ Its first President was Abraham Lincoln.

4. ___ Its first President was Andrew Johnson.

5. ___ It is generally more liberal than the other party.

6. ___ Its members usually prefer to spend tax money for military purposes rather than for social programs.

7. ___ Its members do not want the government to control the lives of individuals.

8. ___ The party symbol is the donkey.

 I **Tell about other political parties in the United States or your native country.**

Module 7B: The Legislative Branch

 A **Work in pairs or groups. Discuss these questions about the legislative branch of the federal government and decide on the answers. Then check your answers on page 8.**

1. What is the legislative branch of U.S. government called?
   a. Congress   b. Parliament

2. What is a "bicameral" legislature?
   a. one with cameras   b. one with two houses (divisions)

3. What are the two houses of Congress?
   a. the Council and the Supreme Soviet   b. the Senate and the House of Representatives

4. Who is President of the Senate? (What is his office?)
   a. Mayor of Washington, D.C.   b. Vice President of the U.S.

5. Who presides if the President of the Senate is absent?
   a. the President pro tempore   b. the Vice President of the U.S.

6. Who presides over the House of Representatives (the House)?
   a. the President of the U.S.   b. the Speaker of the House

7: What party does the Speaker of the House usually belong to?
   a. no political party   b. the majority political party

B Facts About Congress

	the Senate	the House
Number of Members	100	435
Number of Members Per State	2	determined by state population
Length of Term	6 years[1]	2 years[1]
Number of Terms	no limit	no limit
Age Requirement	at least 30	at least 25
Citizenship at least Requirement	9 years as a U.S citizen	at least 7 years as a U.S. citizen
Dates of Regular Session	January 3 to adjournment	January 3 to adjournment

[1] One-third of all Senators and all Representatives run for office every two years.

C Make sentences about the information in B with these sentence patterns.

1. The | Senate / House of Representatives | has _____ members.
(number)

2. The number of | Senators / Representatives | for each state is _____.

3. Each | Senator / Representative | serves in Congress for _____ years.
(number)

4. There is _____ on the number of terms for each | Senator. / Representative.

5. To run for Congress, a | Senator / Representative | must be at least _____ years old
(number)

   and a U.S. citizen for at least_____ years.
   (number)

6. A regular session of the | Senate / House | is from _____ to _____.
(date)

D Write the words from the chart on the next page.

1. To begin the law-making process, either a __**Senator**__ or a _____ can write a _____.

2. The bill then goes to a _____ of the same house.

3. The committee can call _____, _____ (postpone) the bill, send it back to the full house without a _____, or _____ (change) the bill.

4. If the Senate or House _____ the bill, it does not become law.

5. If the Senate or House _____ the bill, it goes to the other house of Congress and its committee.

6. If the second house passes the bill, it goes to _____.

7. If the President signs the bill, it _____.

8. If the President _____ (rejects) the bill, Congress can _____ the veto, and it becomes law anyway.

HOW CONGRESS MAKES LAWS

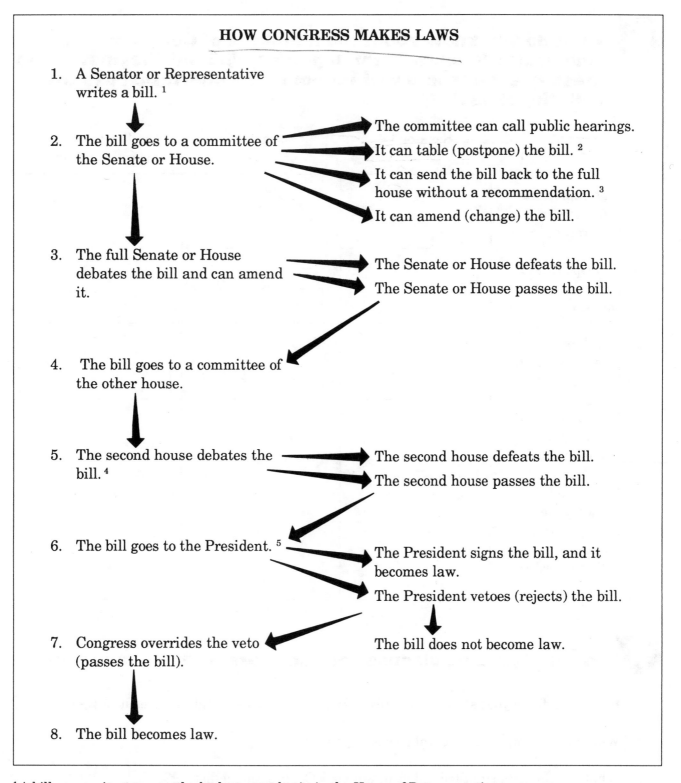

1. A Senator or Representative writes a bill. [1]

2. The bill goes to a committee of the Senate or House.

   The committee can call public hearings.

   It can table (postpone) the bill. [2]

   It can send the bill back to the full house without a recommendation. [3]

   It can amend (change) the bill.

3. The full Senate or House debates the bill and can amend it.

   The Senate or House defeats the bill.

   The Senate or House passes the bill.

4. The bill goes to a committee of the other house.

5. The second house debates the bill. [4]

   The second house defeats the bill.

   The second house passes the bill.

6. The bill goes to the President. [5]

   The President signs the bill, and it becomes law.

   The President vetoes (rejects) the bill.

   The bill does not become law.

7. Congress overrides the veto (passes the bill).

8. The bill becomes law.

[1] A bill concerning taxes or the budget must begin in the House of Representatives.

[2] If a committee tables a bill, Senators or Representatives can force it out of committee with a majority vote.

[3] This step often "kills" the bill.

[4] If the second house of Congress amends the bill, the first house must agree to the changes.

[5] If the President does nothing and Congress adjourns within ten days, the bill does not become law.

What do you know about the members of Congress from your state? In pairs or small groups, find out the answers to these questions and write them in the chart. Discuss them with the class.

	Senator 1	Senator 2	the Representative for your district
1. Who represents your state in Congress? [1]			
2. What political party does he or she belong to?			
3. How long has he or she served in Congress?			
4. Is he or she a "liberal" or a "conservative?"			
5. How do you know? (Give examples from his or her voting record.) [2]			

F   In small groups, discuss your answers to these questions.

1. How powerful is your state in Congress? (How many Representatives does it have?)

2. What are the important federal issues in your state?

3. What are the important federal issues in your Congressional district?

[1] Both Senators represent the whole state. A Representative represents one Congressional district.

[2] You can get information about the voting records of members of Congress from their local offices and from past issues of your local newspaper.

Answers to Exercise A: 1. a 2. b 3. b 4. b 5. a 6. b 7. b

Module 7C: The Executive Branch

 Work in pairs. Look only at this page and ask your partner these questions about the President of the United States. Your partner will tell you the answers from the next page. Take notes on the information.

1. What are the qualifications (requirements) for President?

2. What are the qualifications for Vice President?

3. For how many years may a President serve?

4. If the President dies, who becomes President?

5. Where does the President live and work?

6. How should people address the President?

B **Work in pairs. Look only at this page and tell your partner the steps in electing a President.**

1. Political parties choose their candidates in state caucuses (conventions) or state primaries (elections).

2. Political parties hold national conventions to choose their candidates for President and Vice President. Convention delegates vote for the choices of the voters in their states.

3. All candidates campaign until election day, the first Tuesday after the first Monday in November. Then the voters make their choices.

4. Electors (members of the Electoral College) cast their votes for President and Vice President. The candidates with the majority (more than half) of the electoral votes win.

5. If no candidate wins the majority of the electoral votes, the House of Representatives chooses the new President.

6. The new President takes office during the inauguration (formal ceremony) on January 20 after the election.

Work in pairs. Look only at this page. To answer your partner's questions about the President, find the information and tell it to your partner. He or she will take notes.

- The President travels a lot, but he or she lives and works at the White House in Washington, D.C.

- The President's term of office is four years, and no President may serve for more than two terms in a row.

- To qualify to serve, the President must be a born U.S. citizen and at least thirty-five years old. He or she must have lived in the United States for at least fourteen years.

- Visitors address him as Mr. President.

- The qualifications for Vice President are the same as the qualifications for President.

- If the President dies, these officials take over the position in this order: the Vice President, the Speaker of the House of Representatives, the President pro tempore of the Senate, the Secretary of State, the other twelve members of the Cabinet.

 Work in pairs. Your partner will tell you the steps in electing a President. Number them 1-6 on the lines in correct order.

_____ Electors (members of the Electoral College) cast their votes for President and Vice President. The candidates with the majority of the electoral votes win.

_____ Political parties hold national conventions to choose their candidates for President and Vice President. Convention delegates vote for the choices of the voters in their states.

_____ The new President takes office during the inauguration (formal ceremony) on January 20 after the election.

_____ If no candidate wins the majority of the electoral votes, the House of Representatives chooses the new President.

_____ All candidates campaign until election day, the first Tuesday after the first Monday in November. Then the voters make their choices.

_____ Political parties choose their candidates in state caucuses (conventions) or state primaries (elections).

C **In your own words, tell the steps in electing a President.**

D The Electoral College

U.S. citizens do not vote on federal laws because the U.S. system of government is a representative democracy, but they do choose the President and Vice President of the United States. However, the system of electing these officials is an indirect one.

When voters choose candidates on election day, they are actually voting for presidential "electors." The numbers of electors in each state is equal to the number of senators and representatives from that state in Congress. Because states with large populations have more representatives than states with fewer people, they have more power in an election. The Electoral College is based on a "winner-take-all" system. The winner of the majority of votes in each state gets all of that state's electoral votes. For example, the candidate with over fifty percent of the popular (total) vote in California gets all of that state's forty-seven votes, even if he or she won with only a small majority.

Because of the Electoral College system, occasionally the candidate with the majority of the popular vote loses the presidential election. This event is unusual, however.

In December the electors meet in their state capitals to cast their votes and send them to the U.S. Senate. On January 6 the members of Congress meet to count the votes.

E Write T for true and F for false. Correct the false sentences.

1. ___ U.S. citizens vote on federal laws, but they can't vote for Presidential or Vice Presidential candidates.

2. ___ Voters choose the President and the Vice President of the United States directly through the popular vote.

3. ___ Large states have more electoral votes than small states because their number of electors depends on the number of senators and representatives from the state in Congress.

4. ___ Candidates receive the same percentage of electoral votes from each state as their percentage of popular vote.

5. ___ Even if a candidate receives forty-nine percent of the votes in a state, he or she "loses" the state (gets no electoral votes) in a "winner-take-all" system.

6. ___ The candidate with the majority of the popular vote can still lose the national election.

7. ___ The electors of the Electoral College meet to cast their votes, and the members of Congress meet to count them.

The Cabinet, the Departments, and the Agencies

It is the responsibility of the executive branch of the federal government to enforce the U.S. Constitution and federal laws. The President is Chief Executive and head of the government. The Vice President, the thirteen Cabinet members (usually called Secretaries) and their Departments, and the federal agencies are also part of the executive branch.

The President chooses the members of his Cabinet (the heads of the departments), and the Senate approves his choices. The fourteen departments are the Departments of:

State	the Interior	Health and	Transportation
the Treasury	Agriculture	Human Services	Education
Defense	Commerce	Housing and Urban	Energy
Justice	Labor	Development	Veterans' Affairs

Many federal agencies provide special services and may be temporary. Some well-known agencies are the the Civil Rights Commission, the Environmental Protection Agency, the Federal Trade Commission (FTC), the National Aeronautics and Space Administration, the United States Postal Service, and the Veterans Administration (VA).

G **Write T for true and F for false. Correct the false sentences.**

1. ____ The executive branch makes laws but does not enforce them.

2. ____ The Vice President, the Chief Executive of government, chooses the members of the Cabinet with the approval of the voters.

3. ____ There are fourteen government departments, and their heads are usually called Secretaries.

4. ____ The State Department, the Department of the Treasury, and the Department of Commerce are some federal agencies.

 Do you remember or can you guess the functions of the officials and the departments and agencies of the executive branch? Complete this sentence in various ways.

EXAMPLE: It is the responsibility of the Department of State to advise the President in foreign policy.

It is the responsibility of _____ to _____.

Module 7D: The Judicial Branch

 Work in groups. Discuss these questions about the judicial branch of the federal government and decide on the answers Then check your answers on the next page.

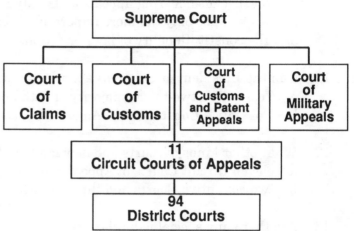

1. What is the highest court of the land?
   a. the Supreme Court
   b. the Presidential Tribunal

2. The Supreme Court is the "Last Court of Appeal." What does this mean?
   a. No other court has higher decision-making power.
   b. Citizens can appeal its decision (take the same case) to lower courts.

3. What does the Supreme Court do?
   a. It approves or overturns decisions of lower courts and explains and interprets laws.
   b. It hears cases from individual citizens without lawyers.

4. In the system of checks and balances, how does the judicial branch have power over the other two branches of government?
   a. The Supreme Court appoints all judges.
   b. The Supreme Court can decide on the constitutionality of laws and Presidential actions.

5. Where is the Supreme Court?
   a. in every state capitol
   b. in Washington, D.C. (the nation's capital)

6. Who chooses the justices of the Supreme Court?
   a. The voters elect them.
   b. The President appoints them, but the Senate must approve them.[1]

7. Who chooses the Chief Justice (head judge) of the Supreme Court?
   a. the President and the Cabinet
   b. The nine justices of the Supreme Court elect him or her.

[1]As an example, in 1987 the Senate rejected President Reagan's candidate, Robert H. Bork, because the Democrats (the majority party) thought he was too conservative.

8. Has there ever been a woman Supreme Court justice?
   a. Yes. Sandra Day O'Connor became the first woman justice in 1981.
   b. No, because the Constitution states that all Supreme Court justices must be men.

9. How long do Supreme Court justices serve?
   a. for the same length of time as senators from their states
   b. for life

10. Must the Supreme Court hear all appeals from lower courts?
    a. Yes, because hearing appeals is its only responsibility.
    b. No. It takes only the more important cases (especially cases concerning individual rights and the constitutionality of laws or actions).

11. Can the President or Congress abolish the Supreme Court?
    a. Yes, with a two-thirds majority of both houses.
    b. No. Only a Constitutional Amendment could abolish it.

12. What other kinds of courts and how many of them are there in the federal system?
    a. eleven Circuit Courts of Appeal and ninety-four District Courts
    b. two Executive Courts and three Legislative Courts

13. Are there any special federal courts?
    a. Yes. There are a Court of Claims, a Court of Customs, a Court of Customs and Patent Appeals, and a Court of Military Appeals.
    b. No. All courts must accept all kinds of cases.

14. What do the Circuit Courts of Appeals do?
    a. They hear appeals (requests to hear the case again) from lower courts.
    b. They overturn decisions of the Supreme Court.

15. What are the District Courts and what happens in them?
    a. They are state courts. All cases concerning state laws begin there.
    b. They are the lowest level of federal courts. Federal cases begin there.

16. How do federal courts differ from other courts?
    a. Federal courts take only cases concerning federal law. Other courts hear cases about state or local law.
    b. There is no difference. All courts take the same kinds of cases.

Answers to Exercise A: 1. a 2. a 3. a 4. b 5. b 6. b 7. b 8. a 9. b 10. b 11. b 12. a 13. a 14. a 15. b 16. a

B Supreme Court Decisions

Supreme Court decisions are very important to the nation because they set precedents. They serve as a guide in law making and the future decisions of all courts. Here are some examples.

Year	Case	Decision
1803	Marbury v. Madison	The Supreme Court has the right to interpret laws and judge their constitutionality.
1824	Gibbons v. Ogden	Only Congress can regulate interstate commerce (trade between states).
1832	Worchester v. Georgia	No state may control Indian Lands.
1941	"Poor Migrants"	It is unconstitutional for states to control or stop migration (movement) of people from one state to another.
1954	Brown v. the Board of Education of Topeka, Kansas	Segregated schools are unconstitutional because they are unequal. Integration (the bringing together of different races) is a part of education.
1963	Gideon v. Wainwright	Even in small cases, the government must provide a lawyer to a defendent (person on trial) if he or she can't afford one.
1964 / 1966	Escobedo v. Illinois / Miranda v. Arizona	The police must tell an arrested person about his or her right to remain silent and to have an attorney (lawyer) present when he or she answers questions.
1971	"Women's Rights"	Unequal treatment based on sex violates (goes against) the Fourteenth Amendment.
1973	Roe v. Wade	States cannot make abortion illegal, except in the later stages of pregnancy.
1981	Rotsker v. Goldberg	Congress may draft (take for military service) only men (not women) into the armed forces.
1982	Plyer v. Doe	Illegal (undocumented) aliens are persons under the Constitution and have the same protections under the law as citizens and residents.
1987	INS v. Cardoza-Fonseca	The U.S. government can give asylum (protection) to refugees if they have reason to fear death or mistreatment in their native countries. Refugees no longer have to prove that their lives are in danger.

C **In groups, read each situation and answer this question: Why would the Supreme Court disapprove of the situation? On the line, write the name and year of the Supreme Court case that is the precedent.**

1. _Plyer v. Doe (1982)_ :
Texas keeps the children of illegal aliens out of its public schools.

2. _____ :
California taxes all goods from Nevada.

3. _____ :
Oregon refuses to let a family move there from Washington because they have no home and little money.

4. _____ :
Arizona sends a woman to jail because she went to the doctor to abort a two-month old fetus.

5. _____ :
Without permission, Nebraska takes land from an Indian reservation to build a state prison.

6. _____ :
A young man refuses to enter the U.S. Army because his sister does not have to serve in the armed forces.

7. _____ :
The police send a man to prison for drunk driving but do not give him an attorney because he can't afford one.

8. _____ :
A public university refuses to admit a student because she is not white.

9. _____ :
You are the best-qualified candidate for police chief but the city won't give you the job you because you are a woman.

10. _____ :
The INS sends a political refugee back to his country because he cannot prove that his government would take his life.

11. _____ :
The police arrest a man and tell him to confess his crime on videotape in a room with no one else present.

12. _____ :
Congress makes the Speaker of the House the head of the armed forces even though the Constitution gives that position to the President.

D **Do you know about other Supreme Court decisions? Tell the class.**

State Government

Module 8A: Branches of Government and Officials

A **Work in pairs. Tell your partner each fact about the federal government and listen to the corresponding fact about state government. Write S on the line if the facts are the same for both governments. Write D if they are different.**

1. _S_ The federal government is in the form of a democratic republic, which means that the people elect representatives.
2. ___ It is a representative democracy because the people have the power through their elected representatives.
3. ___ The government follows the principles of a constitution with its bill of rights.
4. ___ The government has three branches with different responsibilities and powers.
5. ___ The legislative branch has two houses that make laws.
6. ___ The upper house is the Senate, and the lower house is the House of Representatives.
7. ___ The leaders of the executive branch are the U.S. President and Vice President.
8. ___ The President appoints the members of the Cabinet. These advisors ("Secretaries") are the heads of federal departments.
9. ___ The judicial branch of the federal government judges cases of federal law.
10. ___ The highest court is the U.S. Supreme Court. There are also circuit courts of appeals and district courts.

B **From the information in A on this page, write the missing words in the boxes.**

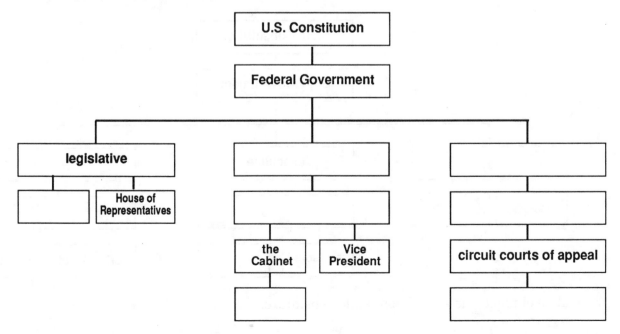

Work in pairs. Tell your partner each fact about state government and listen to the corresponding fact about the federal government. Write S on the line if the facts are the same for both governments. Write D if they are different.

1. __S__ State government is in the form of a democratic republic, which means that the people elect representatives.

2. ___ In addition to power through their elected state representatives, the people have direct power through the initiative, referendum, and recall processes.

3. ___ The government follows the principles of a constitution with its bill of rights.

4. ___ The government has three branches with different responsibilities and powers.

5. ___ The legislative branch has two houses that make laws.*

6. ___ The upper house is a senate, and the lower house is a state assembly or a house of representatives.

7. ___ The leaders of the executive branch are the governor and the lieutenant governor.

8. ___ The executive branch includes advisors to the governor. Some advisors are elected and some are appointed.

9. ___ The judicial branch of state government judges cases of state law.

10. ___ The highest court is the state supreme court. There may also be appellate (appeals), county, superior, district, circuit, municipal, and special courts.

C **From the information in A on this page, write the missing words in the boxes.**

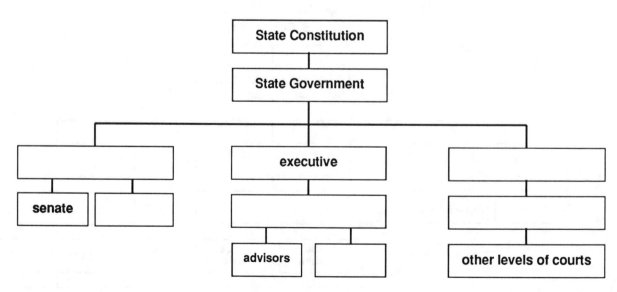

* Only Nebraska has a one-house state legislature.

Make sentences about the similarities and differences in federal and state government with these sentence patterns.

EXAMPLES: 1. Both the federal and state governments are in the form of a republic. In both the federal and state governments, the people elect representatives.

2. Both the federal and state governments are representative democracies because the people elect representatives. On the other hand, in state government, the people also have direct power in law making.

1. (In) Both the federal and state governments _____.

2. (In) The federal government _____.

   On the other hand, (in) state government _____.

E **Read the information. Then find out the answers to the questions about the legislative branch of government in your state.**

Like the Congress of the United States, most state legislatures are bicameral because they consist of two houses, an upper and a lower one. A government leader such as the lieutenant governor or the speaker of the assembly presides over each house.

In some states, citizens elect legislators by population, so there is one representative for a certain number of people. In other states, all voters choose all representatives, so they are elected "at large." In still other states, elections are by district, and there are a certain number of representatives for each geographical area.

1. If you live in a state other than Nebraska, what is the name of the lower house of your state legislature (the house of representatives or the assembly)?

2. What state official presides over each house?

3. How do citizens in your state elect representatives (by population, by district, or "at large")?

4. How long is a term of office in each house?

5. How many members are there in each house?

6. Who are the state legislators from your area? What political parties do they belong to?

Read the information. Then find out the answers to the questions about the executive branch of government in your state.

The chief executive of a state is the governor. A lieutenant governor replaces the governor if he or she can no longer serve. In some states, the governor appoints his or her advisors, and in other states, the people elect them. High state officials may have different titles, but their responsibilities are similar in all states. For example, the Secretary of State keeps records and announces new laws. The Attorney General represents the state in court. The Treasurer receives tax money and pays bills for the state, and the Auditor or Comptroller is concerned with state financial matters. The Superintendant of Public Instruction is the highest officer in educational matters.

1. Who are the governor and lieutenant governor of your state? What political party do they belong to?

2. How long is their term of office? How many terms may they serve?

3. Name five high offices in the executive branch of your state. Are they elected or appointed positions?

4. Who holds the five positions? What do these officers do?

G **Find out the answers to these questions about the supreme court in your state. Then look at the chart and circle the names of the other courts in the judicial branch.**

1. In what city or cities does the state supreme court meet?

2. How many judges are there in the state supreme court? Does the governor appoint them, or do the people elect them?

3. For how many years do they serve?

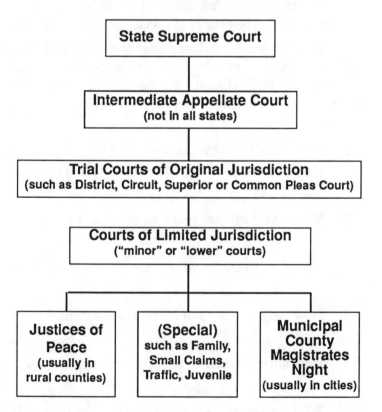

Module 8B: **Functions, Powers, and Services**

A **Work in pairs. Look only at this page and answer your partner's questions about the responsibilities of the federal and state governments.**

Only the federal government:
- declares war
- supports the armed forces
- coins money
- establishes and maintains post offices
- gives authors and inventors the exclusive right to their work (copyrights or patents)
- makes treaties with the governments of other countries

Only a state government:
- maintains a police force
- supports a state militia, such as the National Guard
- regulates transportation and trade within the state
- establishes and maintains schools
- oversees local governments and grants city charters

Both the federal and state governments:
- fund public projects (buildings, dams, highways, etc.)
- support farming and business
- maintain court systems
- regulate banks

The federal government usually provides funding and the states distribute the money and provide programs for:
- public assistance for people in need
- health care
- protection of natural resources
- improvements in living and working conditions

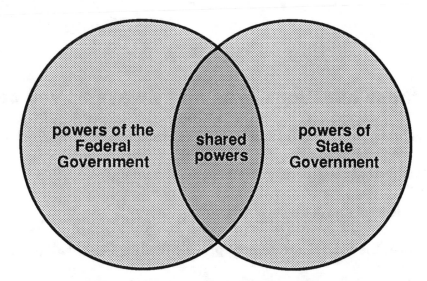

"The powers not delegated to the United States by the Constitution nor prohibited by it to the states are reserved to the states respectively, or to the people." The Tenth Amendment to the Constitution of the United States.

Work in pairs. Look only at this page and ask your partner questions with the pattern "Which government . . .s   . . .?" Write the answer or answers on the line.

EXAMPLE: Student 1: Which government declares war and makes treaties?

Student 2: The federal government.

1.   . . . declares war and makes treaties? _____ *federal* _____

2.   . . . maintains a police force and state militia? _____

3.   . . . regulates trade and transportation in the state? _____

4.   . . . coins money and maintains post offices? _____

5.   . . . establishes and maintains schools? _____

6.   . . . regulates banks and supports business? _____

7.   . . . oversees local government and grants city charters? _____

8.   . . . funds public projects, like dams and highways? _____

9.   . . . maintains court systems? _____

10.   . . . issues copyrights and patents? _____

11.   . . . provides public assistance and health care for people in need?

_____

12.   . . . provides funding for the protection of natural resources?

_____

13.   . . . distributes money through programs to improve living and working conditions?

_____

B   Answer these questions in as many ways as you can.

1.   What can the federal government do that a state government can't? (Example: declare war).

2.   What does a state do that the federal government doesn't do?

3.   What do both the federal and state governments do?

4.   What programs does the federal government provide funding for and state governments maintain?

C The Separation of Powers in State Government

State governments are similar in structure to each other and to the federal government. Under the principle of separation of powers, the government of each state has three branches—the legislative, the executive, and the judicial. In the system of checks and balances, each branch has some control over the other two branches.

The governor may veto bills from the legislature (the senate and the house or assembly). In some states, the governor uses a "line-item veto." This way, he or she does not have to reject an entire law in order to veto parts of it. The governor also appoints judges in the judicial branch. With enough votes in both houses, the legislature can override the governor's veto.

Like the federal courts, state courts also explain and interpret laws. They can declare state laws unconstitutional (contradictory to the state constitution).

State government includes a system of direct democracy. Through the initiative process, citizens may put proposed laws on the ballot for the people to vote on. They may decide on proposed constitutional amendments or important state issues in a referendum. Through a recall, they can sometimes remove an elected government official from office.

The federal government also has power over state governments. For example, a state constitution or court may not contradict the U.S. Constitution, and the U.S. Supreme Court may overrule the decision of a state supreme court. Also, the U.S. President may withhold money from a state if the state refuses to obey federal laws.

D Write T for true and F for false. Correct the false sentences.

1. ___ All state governments are similar to one another, but they are different in structure from the federal government.

2. ___ The principles of separation of powers and checks and balances apply to state as well as the federal government.

3. ___ In a "line-item veto," the governor can reject parts of initiatives, referendums, or recalls.

4. ___ Like in the federal government, state legislatures can override vetos, and state courts can declare laws unconstitutional.

5. ___ Citizens may propose laws, vote on constitutional amendments, and recall elected officials in the federal system of direct democracy but not in a state system.

6. ___ The U.S. Supreme Court and the U.S. President have some direct power over state governments.

How to Find Public Services

The executive branch of state government includes many offices (departments, commissions, and boards) to help the public. You can find their names, addresses, and telephone numbers in the front part of the white pages of your local telephone book. Here are examples from Los Angeles, California:

ALCOHOLIC BEVERAGE CONTROL DEPT
Licensing--Enforcment--Information
El Monte District 9350 Flair Dr
Rm 204..575-6901

ASSEMBLY
Assembly Speaker Willie L. Brown Jr.
107 S Broadway................................620-4356

Alatorre Richard Assemblyman 55th
District 6801 N Figueroa 255-7111

CALIFORNIA COMMUNITY COLLEGES
107 S Broadway 620-2388

CONSUMER AFFAIRS DEPT OF
See White Pages under Consumer
Complaint and Protection Coordinators

CONTRACTORS STATE LICENSE BOARD
7100 Bowling Dr Sacramento
Suite 350....................................916 445-3458

EMPLOYMENT DEVELOPMENT DEPARTMENT
Job Service Downtown Los Angeles
Avalon 161 W Venice Bl 744- 2018

FRANCHISE TAX BOARD
Los Angeles Office 3200 Wilshire Bl

HOUSING AND EMPLOYMENT DISCRIMINATION
322 W 1st. 620-2610

MOTOR VEHICLES DEPT
8 AM To 5 PM Mon-Tue-Wed-Fri
8 AM To 6 30 PM Thur
Alhambra..575-8611
Bell..744-2000
Beverly Hills 271-4585

SOCIAL SERVICES DEPT OF
Public Inquiry & Response--Welfare
Complaints 107 S Broadway 620-4730
Welfare Client Assistance
No Charge to Calling Party 800 952-5253

 Can you guess which state offices can help you solve these problems? In groups, decide on the California department, commission, or board to call in these situations.

1. You need help with state income tax forms.

2. You want information about a bill before it goes before the state assembly.

3. You want to complain about false advertising.

4. You want information about educational opportunities in public two-year colleges.

5. You and your neighbors want to complain about a local liquor store that sells beer to high school students.

6. You believe that it is difficult for your family to rent an apartment because you are from another country.

7. You need to find a job.

8. Your children want to apply for driver's licenses.

9. You need financial help because you have children and no job?

10. You need a license to become a building contractor.

 In your local telephone book, find the names, addresses, and telephone numbers of the state offices to contact in the situations in F. Then discuss the purposes of other listed state departments, commissions, and boards.

Local Government

Module 9A: County and City Services

A Public Services

The names of the departments of county or city government may vary. However, in both large cities and small towns, these departments provide similar services to the public.

B Work in groups of five. Each of you studies the information in a different section. In turn, summarize the information in your own words for the group.

1.

In some cities, there are separate police and fire departments. But in other places, the Department of Public Safety includes a police bureau and a fire bureau.

In the police bureau, there may be a separate traffic division responsible for accident investigation, a detective division to examine the evidence in crimes, and an identification and laboratory section. Volunteer companies may fight fires in the county and in small towns, but the fire bureau of a city is a large professional unit.

2.

The Department of Public Safety may include a building inspector and a traffic engineer. The office of the building inspector issues construction permits to contractors. It sends out employees to inspect new and old buildings. These officials check for violations of the building code, the local rules for safety.

Employees of the city's traffic engineering bureau study traffic patterns and recommend places for one-way streets, traffic lights, stop signs, and so on.

3.

The Public Works Department is responsible for the maintenance of streets and sewers (pipes that carry wastes). Its employees clean the streets and collect garbage. Most cities hire private contractors for major construction projects and repairs.

The Department of Public Utilities usually provides water, gas, and electricity, and in some places, it runs transportation lines. It also operates water purification plants. Employees of the department read the utility meters on each building to determine monthly billing.

4.

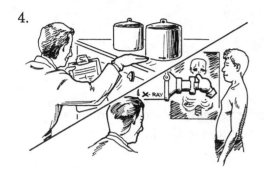

The Department of Public Health sends inspectors out to restaurants, food-processing plants, nursing homes, and similar places. If a place has violated local health or sanitation laws, the department issues warnings and instructions. It can impose penalties if violations are not corrected.

Other divisions of the health department run clinics that provide low-income people with free health services, such as chest X-rays, lab tests, and baby care. They may also offer health education.

5.

The Department of Social Services is concerned with the welfare of people who need help, such as young children, the disabled, the elderly, and the blind. Most of the money for these programs comes from state and federal tax funds.

The Department of Parks and Recreation maintains parks and other recreational facilities, such as community centers, swimming pools, tennis courts, and baseball fields. It may also provide recreational programs (instruction in sports, dances, classes, etc.).

C   Correct these false sentences.

1.   The services of local government departments differ from one city to another, but the names are always the same.

2.   The Department of Public Safety may include social services and health inspection.

3.   Volunteers run the fire departments or bureaus of large cities.

4.   Most cities hire private contractors for minor maintenance of streets and sewers and for garbage collection.

5.   The Department of Public Health has no power because it can't impose penalties for violations of sanitation laws.

6.   The disabled, the elderly, and the blind provide funding for the programs of the Department of Social Services.

Work in pairs. Ask and answer questions about public services with these sentence patterns.

EXAMPLE: Student 1: What does the traffic division of the police department do?

Student 2: It investigates accidents.

1. What | does | _____ usually do?
         | do | (department, division, or people)

2. It | _____ .
    They | (description of service)

E What Can You Learn at City Hall?

Many cities offer guided tours of their seat of government, usually the city or town hall. You can also visit the local departments on your own to find out what they do. Here are some examples of questions you might ask.

The Finance Department

1. How much does it cost to run the city?

2. How does the city spend its money?

3. Where does the money come from?

4. How does the city borrow money?

The Law Department

1. What legal services does the city need?

2. In what situations must the city go to court?

3. What records does the city keep?

4. Can citizens sue the city? (If so, how?)

Transportation Department

1. What public transportation does the city provide?

2. Where does the city get transportation equipment?

3. How does the city plan its systems?

4. How does it get funding for those systems?

The Commerce Department

1. How does the city attract new businesses?

2. What does the city offer visitors and tourists?

3. What public information services does the city offer?

4. How does the city "compete" with other cities?

The City Planning Department

1. How does the city plan its growth?

2. What is zoning, and how does the city use it?

3. What does the city require from private developers?

4. What is the "Master Plan" of the city?

Personnel Department

1. How many employees work for the city?

2. How did they get their jobs?

3. What is the Civil Service system?

4. What is the salary range for city jobs?

As a class or in small groups, visit city hall or the seat of government in your town or county. Complete one or more of these activities and report on your experiences to the class.

1. List the names of the city departments. Circle the departments with the same names as the departments mentioned in this module.

2. Choose one or more of the departments discussed in Exercise B. List at least four questions about it, similar to the questions in E. Visit the department and ask an employee the questions. If you think of more questions, ask them. Take notes on the answers. Summarize the information in a short report.

3. Choose one or more of the departments in E. Visit the department and ask an employee the questions. When he or she gives an interesting answer, ask more questions about that topic. Take notes and summarize the information in a short report.

4. Follow the instructions in (2) for another government department.

G   How to Find Public Services

You can find the names, addresses, and telephone numbers of government offices in the front part of the white pages of your local telephone book. The offices are usually in a list under the title "City Government Offices" or "County Government Offices" and the name of the city or county. Here are examples from a city near Los Angeles, California.

WEST HOLLYWOOD CITY OF

GENERAL INFORMATION	854-7400
CITY CLERK	854-7408
Domestic Partnership Information-Election Info	854-7408
CITY COUNCIL	854-7460
CITY HALL 8611 Santa Monica Bl LA	854-7400
CITY MANAGER	854-7427
CITY CHANNEL 36	854-7388
COMMUNITY DEVELOPMENT	854-7475
Building & Safety	854-7320

Code Enforcement	854-7475
Economic Development	854-7475
Housing	854-7475
Planning & Zoning	854-7475
Transportation	854-7475
FINANCE DIVISION	854-7451
HUMAN SERVICES	854-7471
AIDS Information	854-7471
Fine Arts	854-7471
Recreation Services	854-7471
Senior Service-Referral	854-7471
Social Services	854-7471
LIBRARY	
Bouchardt Senior Citizens Library 1200 N Vista LA	851-8447
PARKS	
Plummer Park 1200 N Vista LA	876-1725
West Hollywood Park	652-3063

PERSONNEL	854-7325
24 Hour Job Hot Line	854-7309
POLICE DEPARTMENT	
Los Angeles County Sheriff West Hollywood Division	
Emergency Calls	911
Business Calls	855-8850
PUBLIC INFORMATION	854-7423
PUBLIC WORKS	854-7327
Contract Administration	854-7327
Engineering	854-7327
Service Requests	854-7327
Traffic Division	854-7327
Bus Pass Information	854-7327
RENT STABILIZATION	854-7450
Administration	854-7450
Hearings	854-7450

Work in pairs. Ask and answer questions with these sentence patterns about the telephone listings in G.

1. What are the divisions or offices of the _____?
                                    (department)

2. What does the _____ usually do?
                   (department or division)

Work in pairs. Repeat Exercise H with the listings for city or county government offices from your local telephone book.

Module 9B: County Government

A The Structure of County Government

County government is different in structure from state and federal government. The elected governing body has many different names throughout the country, but "board of supervisors" and "board of county commissioners" are two common ones.

A county board receives its authority from the county charter (official document to establish an organization). It not only passes ordinances (county laws), but it enforces them, too, along with state laws. The board may share executive powers with other elected officials such as the sheriff. County revenue comes from the federal and state governments, county property taxes, and other sources such as sales and income taxes and licensing.

A small county board has between five and eleven elected members, usually part-time officials. They meet in the county seat, a city or town in the county.

B Here is some information about state government. Finish each sentence with the corresponding information about county government.

1. The elected governing body of the state is the state legislature, but the elected governing body of the county _has many different names, such as "board of supervisors"_.

2. The state government receives its authority from the state constitution, but the county board
    _____.

3. The state legislature passes state laws, but the county board
    _____.

4. The governor is the chief executive of the state, but the county board
    _____.

5. State revenue comes from state taxes, but county revenue
    _____.

6. The state legislature has hundreds of members, but a county board
    _____.

7. State legislators usually meet in the state capital, but county board members
    _____.

C   Other County Officials

In some counties, the voters elect officials, and in other counties, the board appoints them. The high officials in many counties have the same level of power as the elected board members. Here are some common titles for officials and their responsibilities.

Official	Responsibilities
County Attorney / District Attorney	• is the lawyer for the county • brings criminal cases to court
Sheriff	• provides police protection • oversees the county jails
Assessor	• determines property values so the county can set tax rates
Treasurer	• receives tax money • pays bills for the county
County Engineer	• plans and manages construction projects
Superintendant of Schools	• oversees county schools not part of city school systems
County Clerk*	• is an official recorder of county business • is secretary to the county board • issues birth certificates and marriage licenses

D   Work in pairs. Ask and answer questions about the responsibilities of county officials with these sentence patterns.

EXAMPLE: Student 1: What does the district attorney usually do?

Student 2: He or she is a lawyer for the county.

1.   What does the _____ usually do?
                          (official)

2.   He | _____.
     She | (description of service)

* In large cities, there may be more than one recording office. In Los Angeles, for example, residents go to the Registrar-Recorder for family documents and voter registration.

E An Example of County Organization

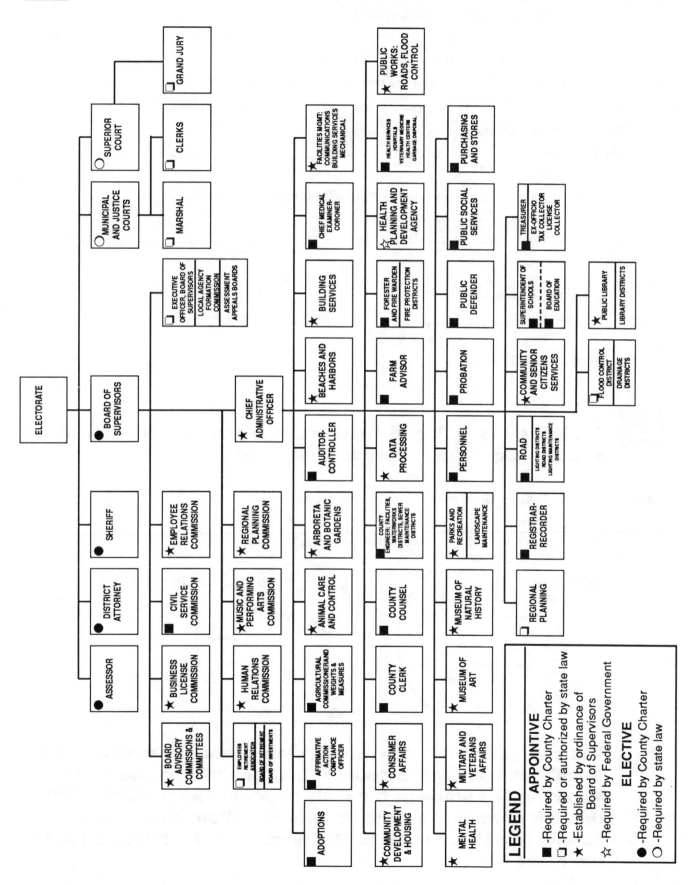

LEGEND

APPOINTIVE

- ■ - Required by County Charter
- □ - Required or authorized by state law
- ★ - Established by ordinance of Board of Supervisors
- ☆ - Required by Federal Government

ELECTIVE

- ● - Required by County Charter
- ○ - Required by state law

Work in pairs. Ask and answer these questions about the chart on the previous page.

1. What officials are elected rather than appointed?

2. What officials have the same level of power as the members of the board of supervisors?

3. What are some examples of appointed positions required by state law? (See the Legend.)

4. What are some examples of high-level commissions?

5. What are some examples of departments or sections under the supervision of the chief administrative officer?

6. What are the special districts (organizations for large, expensive responsibilities)?
   _____

7. Which is higher on the organizational chart: (the) _____ or (the)
                                                         (official or office)
   _____?}
     (official or office)

8. What does (the) _____ usually do?
                    (official or office)

9. (a question of your own)

 Work in pairs. Ask and answer questions with this question pattern about the county budget charts.

EXAMPLE: What percentage of county revenue comes from the state?

What percentage of county | revenue expenditures | comes from goes to | _____?

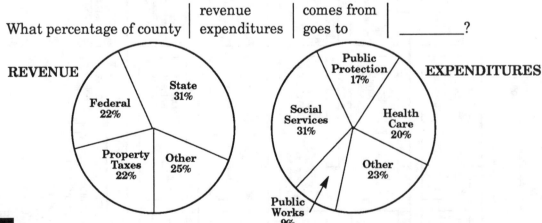

REVENUE

State 31%
Federal 22%
Property Taxes 22%
Other 25%

EXPENDITURES

Public Protection 17%
Social Services 31%
Health Care 20%
Other 23%
Public Works 9%

 You can get information about your county from your local telephone book and a county "fact book" from the public library or the office of the district county supervisor. With this information, ask and answer questions about your county like those in F and G. Summarize the information for the class.

Module 9C: City Government

A The Structure of City Government

The government of a state grants city charters, and the charter establishes the form of local government. There are three main forms.

Law-Making Body	How Chosen?	Chief Executive	How Chosen?	Functions and Powers
city council	elected by the people	the mayor	elected by the people	may have actual power or be only a council member[1]
city council	elected	the city manager	hired by council	takes instructions from the council
commission	elected	one commissioner	chosen by commission	is the ceremonial head of government only[2]

B Make sentences about the information in A with these sentence patterns.

EXAMPLE: The city charter establishes the mayor-council form of government.

1. In one form of city government, the members of the _____ are
                                                              (law-making body)

    _____ by the voters.
     (how chosen?)

2. The chief executive, _____, is _____.
                              (title of official)   (how chosen?)

3. He or she _____.
                        (functions and powers)

C Make sentences about the form of government in your town or city with the patterns in B. Begin Sentence 1 with "In our form of city government, ..."

[1]In some cities, the mayor carries out the laws and is the most powerful local government leader. In other cities, the mayor is simply a council member who represents the city in ceremonies.

[2]All the commissioners are executive officers of the city, and one is the ceremonial head.

Getting Involved in Local Government

In many countries, the national or central government runs the cities through its officials. But in the United States, local government means self-government. The state government creates cities and determines their responsibilities and powers, and no city council or commission may contradict its charter or state law. But the city may have a large amount of freedom, and every resident of the city has the opportunity to participate directly in local government.

 Correct these false sentences.

1. In the United States, the national government runs the cities through its officials.

2. The city council or commission can contradict its charter and state law in local matters because cities create themselves.

3. City residents cannot participate directly in local government because cities have no self-government.

 Walk around the classroom and ask your classmates these questions about their experiences in the United States and their native countries. When someone answers *yes*, write his or her name on the line. Then ask questions and write notes on the answers.

Have you or someone you know ever. . .

1. . . . .run for local political office (Example: on a board of a special district)?

_____

2. . . .supported a local candidate for office (Examples: by calling, visiting voters, or contributing money)? _____

3. . . .attended a city council, commission, or board meeting or heard one on the radio?

_____

4. . . .supported or opposed a local issue? (How?) _____

5. . . .joined a public protest, such as a street demonstration? _____

G **City residents can make important changes through neighborhood action. Divide the class into groups of "neighbors." Each group chooses a different one of the following local issues. Discuss the situation and suggest three or more solutions. Then tell the class your solutions and the reasons for them. The class will decide on the best one.**

1. There have been many accidents on the corner of your street because there is no stop sign.

2. Rainwater doesn't drain well on your street, and the street sweeper doesn't clean the street well because not all residents move their cars.

3. There have been several burglaries in your neighborhood recently, and you are especially afraid because your street is very dark at night.

4. You know that some residents in your building sell drugs, but you are afraid to call the police.

5. You live downtown and always see homeless people sleeping on the streets at night. The rents in the area are high.

6. Teenagers from the local high school cruise the main boulevard every Friday and Saturday night. They often get into fights, damage property, and write graffiti on walls.

7. (a situation of your own)

The Board of Education

In some places, the city council appoints the board of education and controls school funding. But in most cities, the board is more independent of local government. It often has its own budget and may collect taxes. Sometimes its members are elected, and board meetings are open to the public.

Board members must make decisions on the many problems that face the school system. The public expresses its opinions in various ways. The views in this letter are typical:

> Dear Members of the Board of Education:
>
> We parents demand changes in the city school system. There are too many students in each classroom and too few teachers and other school personnel to control them. Our schools are becoming dangerous. Why don't school principals expel students who disturb classes so that our children can learn? Our sons and daughters score low on national tests, but they seldom have homework to do. If the situation does not improve soon, this parents' organization will sponsor a petition to recall the school board members and elect new ones.
>
> Parents for Better Education

 In small groups, pretend that you are members of the local school board. Discuss your answers to these questions. Together, write an answer to the letter in H.

1. How much money is available for new teachers and other school personnel?
2. Are there classrooms available for more (smaller) classes? If not, how much money is available for new rooms or schools?
3. How might the community raise more money for education?
4. In the United States, every child has the right to a free public education. Can school principals expel students?
5. Are national test scores important? If so, how can teachers improve the scores of their students?
6. Should students have homework? If so, how much?
7. What are the responsibilities of parents in the education of their children?

The History of the United States

Module 10A: Overview of U.S. History

A Ten Periods of U.S. History

1.  Christopher Columbus discovered North America. European explorers and settlers came to the new land for gold, adventure, and freedom. The colonists lived under British laws.

| 1492 |
| 1500's |
| 1600's |

2.  Americans in the thirteen colonies wanted to be free of British rule. General George Washington led the colonists in the Revolutionary War. Thomas Jefferson wrote the Declaration of Independence, and the colonies approved it.

| 1775 |
| 1776 |

3.  The American colonists won the war, and the colonies became the United States of America. The Constitution became the highest law of the land, and George Washington became the first President.

| 1783 |
| 1787 |
| 1789 |

4. 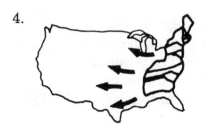 Millions of Europeans came to America as workers during the Industrial Revolution. The new nation grew and added more states. It expanded to the Pacific Ocean.

| 1840's |
| 1853 |

5.  Americans fought against one another in the Civil War between the North and the South. President Abraham Lincoln freed the slaves in the Emancipation Proclamation. The northern states won the war, and the period of Reconstruction (rebuilding) began.

| 1861 |
| 1863 |
| 1865 |

6.

The United States grew to be one of the great powers in the world. The nation fought in the First World War. After the war women got the right to vote for the first time.

1917

1920

7.

The Great Depression began with the stock market crash. Banks, factories, and farms shut down, and many Americans were unemployed. President Franklin Roosevelt helped end the Depression with the New Deal government.

1929

1933

8.

The United States entered the Second World War when Japan attacked the Hawaiian Islands. The war ended when the United States dropped the first atomic bombs, and the world entered the Nuclear Age.

1941

1945

9.

Because of its distrust of and competition with the Soviet Union and other Communist nations, the United States entered a time of Cold War. Americans fought in the Korean War. The Civil Rights Movement began, and black and white Americans fought against segregation (separation of the races).

1950's

10.

The Space Age began. Americans fought in the Vietnam War. The United States put the first men on the moon in the Apollo Program. The Women's Liberation Movement became strong. Computers began to change the nation faster than ever before.

1960's

1970's

1980's

B Write the dates from the box.

| 1853   1776   1955   1863   1919   1929   1492   1941   1787   1969 |

1. Columbus discovered North America in _**1492**_ .
2. The colonies approved the Declaration of Independence in _____.
3. The Constitution became the law of the land in _____.
4. The United States expanded to the Pacific Ocean by _____.
5. President Lincoln freed the slaves in _____.
6. The First World War ended in _____.
7. The Great Depression began in _____.
8. The United States entered the Second World War in _____.
9. The Civil Rights Movement began in _____.
10. The United States put the first men on the moon in _____.

C Number the events in each group in time order 1-3.

1. _2_ The time of Reconstruction began.
   _3_ Banks shut down, and many Americans were unemployed.
   _1_ The colonies wanted to be free of British rule.

2. ___ General Washington led the colonists in the Revolutionary War.
   ___ European workers came to America during the Industrial Revolution.
   ___ George Washington became the first President of the United States.

3. ___ The northern states won the Civil War.
   ___ Americans fought in the Vietnam War.
   ___ Americans fought in the Korean War.

4. ___ Americans began to fight against segregation.
   ___ President Roosevelt established the New Deal government.
   ___ The United States entered the First World War.

Write T for true and F for false. Correct the false sentences.

1. ___ After Columbus discovered North America, European settlers lived in the colonies under British rule.

2. ___ England won the Revolutionary War against the American colonies.

3. ___ The Declaration of Independence became the highest law of the land.

4. ___ George Washington was the first President of the United States.

5. ___ Millions of native American Indians came to the United States as workers during the Industrial Revolution.

6. ___ Americans from the northern and southern states fought against one another during the First World War.

7. ___ President Abraham Lincoln freed the slaves with the Mayflower Compact.

8. ___ Women didn't have the right to vote in the United States until after the First World War.

9. ___ The Great Depression began with the Second World War.

10. ___ The Depression ended after Franklin Roosevelt became President and established the New Deal government.

11. ___ The United States fought against Japan in the Second World War and dropped the first atomic bombs.

12. ___ During the time of the "Cold War," the United States and the Communist Soviet Union were good friends.

13. ___ In the Civil Rights Movement Americans fought against segregation of black and white people.

14. ___ America stayed out of the Korean and the Vietnam Wars.

15. ___ In the Space Age the Women's Liberation Movement became strong.

Work in groups of five or more. One student makes a sentence (tells a fact) about the Exploration and Colonization period of American history. The second student repeats the first student's sentence or corrects it if necessary. He or she tells a fact about the American Revolution. The third student repeats or corrects the second student's sentence and makes a new sentence about the New Nation, and so on for all ten periods of American history.

Module 10B: Exploration and Colonization

A Exploration

1.  In 1492 Christopher Columbus was trying to find a way from Europe to the Far East. But he didn't get to China. Instead, he found some islands in the Atlantic Ocean near North America. He thought he was near the Indies, so he called the people Indians. The Indians were native Americans. By accident, this sailor from Spain discovered a new world.

2.  Soon other European explorers sailed across the Atlantic to learn about this exciting discovery. The Spanish explored South America in search of adventure and gold. Priests came to teach the native people.

3.  The British and the French explored North America. Explorers traveled into the land and discovered many beautiful forests, valleys and rivers.

B Match the sentence parts. Write the letters on the lines.

1. C Christopher Columbus
2. A The Indians
3. E European explorers
4. B The Spanish
5. D Priests
6. F The British and the French

a. were native Americans

b. explored South America to find adventure and gold.

c. wanted to sail to China but discovered North America.

d. came to teach the Indians.

e. crossed the Atlantic to learn about the New World.

f. explored the land of North America.

C Colonization

1.  The Spanish established the first permanent settlement in North America. It was St. Augustine, now in the state of Florida. The British established their first permanent settlement at Jamestown, Virginia, in 1607.

2.  People from Spain, France, Holland, England, and other countries started other villages on the east coast of North America. Thirteen settlements became colonies of England. They were Virginia, Massachusetts, Maryland, Rhode Island, Connecticut, New Hampshire, North and South Carolina, New York, New Jersey, Pennsylvania, Delaware, and Georgia.

3.  Some of the native people were friendly to the colonists and taught them about the land. But other Indians attacked them. The settlers killed many Indians and took their land. They pushed the Indians to the West.

D Write T for true and F for false. Correct the false sentences.

1. _F_ The British established the first permanent settlement in North America at St. Augustine, Florida.

2. _F_ The first Spanish settlement was at Jamestown, Virginia, in 1607.

3. _F_ Thirteen European settlements on the east coast became colonies of Spain and France.

4. _F_ Some of the settlers were friendly to the native Americans and taught them about the land.

5. _T_ The colonists killed many Indians and pushed them to the West.

E The Thirteen Original Colonies

Colony	Reasons for Establishment	Some Facts
1. Virginia	to find gold and to trade with Europe	The colonists wanted to be rich. They didn't want to do the difficult work to live, and many people died. Then the settlers discovered tobacco and used it for trade.
2. Massachusetts	for religious freedom	The Pilgrims came to Plymouth in 1620. The Puritans established the Massachusetts Bay Colony. They came for religious freedom, but they didn't give the same freedom to other churches.
3. Maryland	to make money from land sales	The King of England gave the land to Lord Baltimore. Lord Baltimore sold the land to settlers. He also gave religious freedom to Catholics.
4. Rhode Island	for religious freedom	Some Puritans left Massachusetts to start a new colony with religious freedom for everyone. They established the principle of separation of church and state (religion and government).
5. Connecticut	for religious freedom and economic reasons	Thomas Hooker and people from his church left Massachusetts for this new colony because the farmland was better.
6. New Hampshire	for religious, political, and economic reasons	Settlers came here from Massachusetts. They lived from fishing and trading.
7. North and South Carolina	for economic reasons	The King of England gave away the land, and the landowners rented it to settlers from Virginia and Europe.
8. New York	for political reasons	Dutch settlers were living in New Netherlands, but the British took the land from them and named it New York.

Colony	Reasons for Establishment	Some Facts
9. New Jersey	to make money from rent	Landowners rented the land to settlers.
10. Pennsylvania	for religious freedom	Willian Penn established this colony. The Quakers settled here and gave religious freedom to everyone.
11. Delaware	for political reasons	William Penn gave settlers from Pennsylvania this land because they wanted a separate government.
12. Georgia	for political and economic reasons	People came here from England because they were in debt (owed money). The government gave them land to farm.

F **Make sentences about the information in E. You can use these sentence patterns.**

EXAMPLE: Settlers established the colony of Virginia to find gold and to trade with Europe. Many settlers died because they didn't work enough.

Settlers established the colony of _____ | for _____ .
| to _____ .
| because _____ .

G **Write the letters from the map on the lines. Then tell one fact about each colony.**

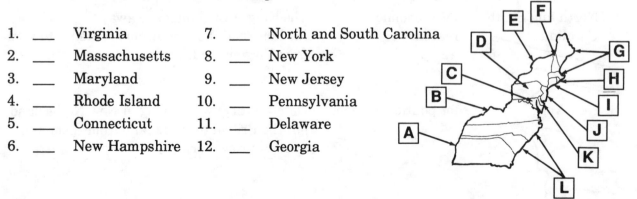

1. ___ Virginia
2. ___ Massachusetts
3. ___ Maryland
4. ___ Rhode Island
5. ___ Connecticut
6. ___ New Hampshire

7. ___ North and South Carolina
8. ___ New York
9. ___ New Jersey
10. ___ Pennsylvania
11. ___ Delaware
12. ___ Georgia

Module 10C: Revolution

A The Causes of the American Revolution

1.  The King of England allowed the thirteen American colonies a large amount of self-government. One of the reasons for this freedom was that between 1689 and 1763 England was busy with wars against France. The colonists helped the Mother Country (England) against the French in the French and Indian War.

2.  In 1763 the war ended, and England won control over most of the colonies of North America. But by this time the colonists felt they were "Americans." They often traded with other countries. They felt strong, and they did not need the Mother Country for protection in wars anymore. They were used to freedom and self-government.

3.  But the English needed the colonies for economic reasons. They were buying goods from the colonies at low prices and selling back manufactured products at high prices. They were also charging high taxes on American trade with other countries. Then England put new taxes on the colonists, such as the Stamp Act (taxes on printed materials).

4.  Other strict laws made life difficult for the colonists. For example, they could send their products only on British ships, and they had to sell some goods only to England at very low prices. British officials could enter homes to search for illegal goods. The colonists were not free to settle west of the Appalachian Mountains, and they had to allow British soldiers to live in their homes.

5.  The colonists were especially angry about the "taxation without representation." They had to pay high taxes but could not send delegates to England to vote on them. In 1773 England passed the Tea Act (taxes on imported tea), so some colonists dressed up like Indians and dumped all the tea from a British ship into Boston harbor. This act was called the Boston Tea Party.

6.  To punish the colonies and control them more closely, England passed even stricter laws. To show their unity against England, the colonies sent representatives to the First Continental Congress in Philadelphia. The Congress decided to stop buying British goods and demanded rights for the colonists in a declaration. Americans prepared for war.

B Here are some causes of the American Revolution. Write B on the lines before the sentences about the British. Write C before the sentences about the colonists.

1. ___ They were used to freedom and self-government and didn't need the Mother Country for protection anymore.

2. ___ They were buying goods at low prices and selling back manufactured products at high prices.

3. ___ Their lives were difficult because of strict laws about trade, settlement, and soldiers.

4. ___ They were angry about "taxation without representation," so they dumped tea from a ship into Boston harbor.

5. ___ To punish and have more control, they passed even stricter laws.

6. ___ To show unity, they met at the First Continental Congress and demanded their rights.

C Match the sentence parts. Write the letters on the lines.

1. ___ The American colonies had a large amount of self-government because

2. ___ England got control over North America because

3. ___ The "Boston Tea Party" occurred because

4. ___ The English passed even stricter laws because

5. ___ The colonies stopped buying British goods and prepared for war because

a. they couldn't get rights from the British.

b. they wanted to punish the colonies for the Boston Tea Party.

c. the colonists couldn't send representatives to England to vote on taxes.

d. the Mother Country was busy with wars at that time.

e. the English won the French and Indian War.

D Events of the Revolutionary War

Date	Places	Some Facts
April 19, 1775	Lexington and Concord, Massachusetts	British soldiers shot at some Minute Men (colonists ready to fight) at Lexington. The colonists fired shots at British soldiers at Concord and began the Revolutionary War.
June 1775	Boston, Massachusetts (Bunker Hill) other colonies	General George Washington led the colonists, but the colonial army did not have enough soldiers, training, or supplies. The British won many battles.
July 4, 1776	Philadelphia, Pennsylvania	Representatives of the Second Continental Congress declared the independence of the colonies from British rule. The Congress adopted the Declaration of Independence.
1778, 1779, 1780	the middle and southern colonies	The colonial army could shoot well, and George Washington gave the soldiers courage. France entered the war on the side of the colonists.
October 19, 1781	Yorktown, Virginia	The colonial army won some important battles and took control.
1783	Paris, France	The war ended. American delegates signed a peace treaty with England. America won land and independence.

Make sentences about the information in D. You can use these sentence patterns.

EXAMPLES: 1. The Revolutionary War began because the British refused to give the American colonists their rights.

2. On April 19, 1775, the British shot at some Minute Men at Lexington, Massachusetts.

1. _____ because _____ .

2. On | _____ , _____ | on | _____ .
   In | (date) | in | (place)

F   **Study the map and write words from it on the lines.**

The United States after the Treaty of Paris (1783)

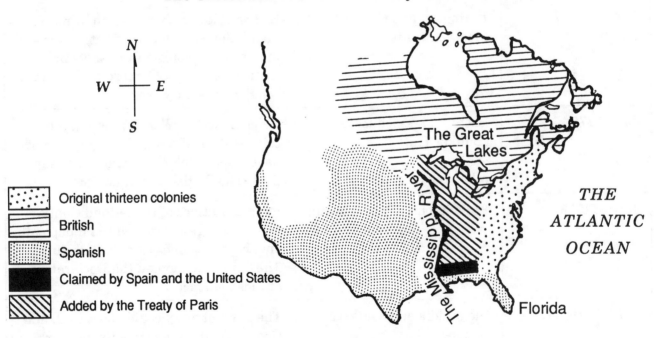

After 1783 the eastern border of the United States was (1) __the Atlantic Ocean__, and the western border was (2) _____ . The (3) _____ controlled (4) _____ and the land west of the Mississippi River. The (5) _____ controlled the land north of (6) _____ .

Module 10D: Growth and Westward Movement

A From the Atlantic to the Pacific in Fifty Years

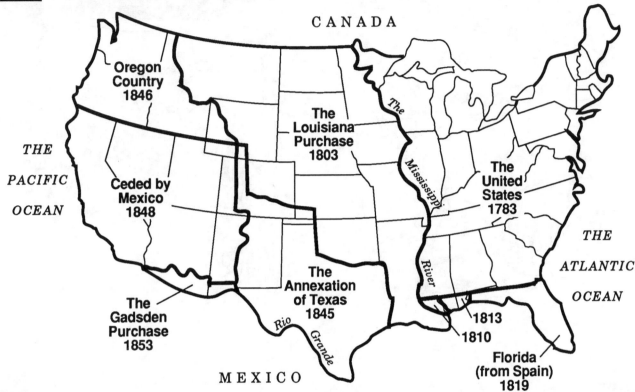

B Finish these sentences with information from the map in A.

After the American Revolution in 1783, the territory of the the United States stretched from

(1) **the Atlantic Ocean** in the East to (2) _____ in the West. In 1803 President

Jefferson bought the territory west of the Mississippi River from France in (3) _____.

In the year (4) _____ the U.S. obtained the land of the state of (5) _____ from Spain.

The U.S. annexed (added) the territory of (6) _____ in 1845. President Polk divided the

large (7) _____ with Great Britain in 1846, and England received the northern half in

Canada. After a war in 1848, (8) _____ ceded (had to give up) the territory from the Louisiana

Purchase to the Pacific Ocean. The U.S. paid $10 million in the year (9) _____ for some Mexican

land in the Southwest, called (10) _____.

C   Moving West in Wagon Trains

D   Circle the correct word or words in each choice. The pictures in C suggest the answers.

Thousands of Americans moved to [1. eastern / (western)] territories to start new lives. Groups of over sixty people traveled in [2. cars / covered wagons]. Six [3. horses / oxen] pulled each wagon across the land and rivers and over hills at about [4. two / sixty] miles per hour, so a 2000-mile trip from Missouri to California took about five [5. hours / months]. No wagon traveled [6. alone / with others]. Wagon trains were important for protection against the [7. British / Indians].

At night, the wagons formed a [8. circle / long line], like a wall around a small town. The men protected the train with [9. guns / bombs]. The travelers had [10. meetings / slaves] and made rules for themselves. Everyone worked together, especially in times of danger.

E Difficult Years in Texas

Before 1836 the Texas area belonged to Spain and then to Mexico. Under the leadership of Stephen Austin, American settlers moved to Texas. The Mexican government wanted these settlers to become Mexican citizens and Roman Catholics and to free their slaves, but the settlers had other ideas. They demanded local self-government and the same rights as Americans in the United States, such as trial by jury.

The settlers declared their independence from Mexico and formed the Republic of Texas. The Mexican army of General Santa Anna defeated the rebels at the Alamo on March 6, 1836. But with the spirit of the battle cry "Remember the Alamo," Sam Houston and the Texans won a battle at San Jacinto on April 21. They signed a peace treaty with Mexican leaders and elected Houston President of the "Lone Star Republic."

The Republic of Texas did not become part of the United States for nine years because most northerners opposed the annexation of another slave state.

F Write T for true and F for false. Correct the false sentences.

1. ___ Before 1836 the area of Texas belonged to England.

2. ___ Stephen Austin was the leader of the Mexican Roman Catholics.

3. ___ The settlers in Texas believed in slavery, demanded local self-government, and wanted the rights of Americans.

4. ___ They wanted to separate from Mexico and form their own republic.

5. ___ Santa Anna was the American military leader, and Sam Houston was a Mexican general.

6. ___ The Texans had the spirit to defeat the Mexican army because they remembered the battle at the Alamo.

7. ___ The "Lone Star Republic" was the Republic of Texas.

8. ___ Jefferson Davis became the President of Texas.

9. ___ Texas became part of the U.S. right away because it was a free state.

Some Principles of the Times

In 1823 President Monroe warned European nations not to interfere with the politics of the Western Hemisphere (North and South America). The Monroe Doctrine was an example of the principle of nationalism. By the 1840's most Americans believed that the United States should expand to the Pacific Ocean because it was their "manifest destiny" (fate). The settlers organized some of the land into "territories," and these later became states. The following states were admitted officially into the Union before the time of the Civil War.

	Became a Territory	Became a State			Became a Territory	Became a State
Vermont		1791		Arkansas	1819	1836
Kentucky		1792		Michigan	1805	1837
Tennessee		1796		Florida	1822	1845
Ohio		1803		Texas		1845
Louisiana	1804	1812		Iowa	1838	1846
Indiana	1800	1816		Wisconsin	1836	1848
Mississippi	1798	1817		California		1850
Illinois	1809	1818		Minesota	1849	1858
Alabama	1817	1819		Oregon	1848	1859
Maine		1820		Kansas	1854	1861
Missouri	1812	1821				

H   **Correct these false sentences.**

1. In the Monroe Doctrine, President Madison warned ~~South American~~ *European* nations not to interfere with the politics of Europe.

2. The doctrine was an example of the principle of separatism.

3. Because of the principle of "taxation without representation," many Americans thought that the U.S. should expand to the Mississippi River.

4. Some of the land became "countries," and these were later admitted into the House of Representatives as states.

I   **Make sentences about the information in G. You can use these sentence patterns.**

1. _____ | was organized as a territory | in _____ .
   (state) | was admitted as a state | (year)

2. _____ became a | territory | before | _____ .
   (state) | state | in the same year as | (state)

Module 10E: The Time of the Civil War

A   The Causes of the Civil War

In the 1800s the northern and the southern states disagreed on basic issues. Their differences led to the Civil War.

The North...	The South...

The North...

...lived from industry and the manufacture of goods such as clothing and furniture. Northern factories did not use slaves. The abolitionists (opponents of slavery) worked to free the slaves.

...produced expensive products and got the U.S. government to put a protectionist tax on products from other countries.

...was adding free states to the Union and had a larger population than the South. The northern states had more representatives in Congress than the southern ones.

...believed in the unity of the United States and opposed the separation of the southern states from the Union.

...supported the election of Abraham Lincoln as President of the United States.

The South...

...depended on agriculture for its economy. The main crop was cotton, and southern planters felt they needed slave workers to make money. They opposed the abolition of slavery.

...preferred cheap European goods to the expensive products of northern factories and opposed the protective tax on them.

...was adding slave states to the Union but had a smaller population than the North. The southern states were losing power in the House of Representatives.

...opposed federal laws and seceded (separated) from the Union by creating the Confederate States of America.

...opposed the election of Lincoln and chose Jefferson Davis President of the Confederacy.

B   Make sentences about the information in A. You can use these sentence patterns and the pictures on the next page for ideas.

1. The northern states _____, but the southern states _____.

2. Although the North _____, the South _____.

3. The states of the North _____. On the other hand, the states of the South _____.

1.

2.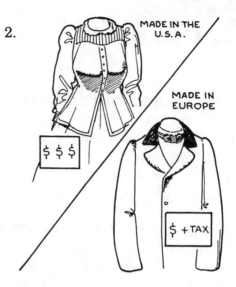

3.

4.

 Finish each sentence about the map on the next page with the names of different states.

EXAMPLE: During the time of the Civil War, the state of Illinois was free, but Tennessee was a slave state.

1. During the time of the Civil War, the state of _____ was free, but _____ was a slave state.

2. The state of _____ seceded from the Union to become part of the Confederacy (the Confederate States of America).

3. Although _____ was a slave state, it did not secede.

Free States

These slave states seceded

These slave states did not secede

The western section of Virginia refused to secede and became a separate state in 1863

D The Strengths of Both Sides in the Civil War

The War Between the States divided not only the country but also families. It was long and difficult because each side had advantages, so the North and the South were about equal in strength.

Both sides had excellent generals: Ulysses S. Grant for the Union and Robert E. Lee for the Confederacy. The North was richer, and its factories supplied its army with weapons. Most of the railroads were in the North, and the Union controlled the U.S. Navy. Supplies for the Confederate army, on the other hand, had to travel only short distances. Its soldiers had more spirit because they were fighting for their own land.

E Write N on the line before each sentence about the North. Write S before each sentence about the South.

1. **N** General Ulysses S. Grant was the military leader.

2. ___ General Robert E. Lee led the army.

3. ___ It got weapons for its army from its own factories.

4. ___ It controlled most of the railroads and the U.S. Navy.

5. ___ Its army got supplies more quickly because they didn't have to travel long distances.

6. ___ Its army was defending its own land, so the soldiers had more spirit.

F   Events of the Civil War

Date	Place	Some Facts
July 1861	Bull Run (near Washington D.C.)	Spectators from Washington came to watch the battle as entertainment. To their surprise, the Confederate army defeated Union forces.
1861 1862	The East The West	Neither side was winning. Then General Grant won many battles and demanded the surrender of the Confederates.
January 1, 1863		In the Emancipation Proclamation, President Abraham Lincoln announced that the slaves in all states under Confederate control were free. The proclamation weakened the spirit of the South.
July 1863	Gettysburg, Pennsylvania	The North won an important battle. Lincoln made a famous speech, the Gettysburg Address, at the battlefield.
1863 1864	Georgia and the Carolinas	The army of General William Sherman marched through the South and destroyed homes, plantations, and railroads. The cruelty of the soldiers destroyed the spirit of the South.
April 3, 1865	Richmond, Virginia	The North captured the Confederate capital. General Lee surrendered at Appomattox Court House. The war was over.

G   Work in pairs or groups. Make sentences about the information in F. You can use this sentence pattern. Your classmates will answer "true" or "false."

EXAMPLES: Student 1:   In July 1861, spectators from Washington, D.C. came to watch a battle at Bull Run.

Student 2:   True. On this day the Union forces defeated the Confederate army as expected.

Student 1:   False. The Confederate forces defeated the Union army, and everyone was surprised.

On	_____ ,	_____	in	_____ .
In	(date)		at	(place)

Module 10F: Industrialization

A **Work in pairs. Look only at this page and ask your partner these questions about the time of Reconstruction. Your partner will tell you the answers from the information on the next page. Write them on the lines.**

1. When was the period of Reconstruction? _____from 1865 to 1877_____

2. How did Republicans of the North help ex-slaves during this time? _____
   _____

3. What did the 13th Amendment to the U.S. Constitution do? _____
   _____

4. What were the 14th and 15th Amendments? _____

5. How did the North punish the South? _____

6. What couldn't former southern leaders do? _____

7. Why didn't white southerners accept the new laws? _____
   _____

8. What happened to the U.S. during the time of Reconstruction? _____
   _____

B **To answer your partner's questions, find the information and tell it to your partner. He or she will write the answers.**

The Industrial Revolution

Before the nineteenth century, people produced most goods by hand. But during the Industrial Revolution, machines changed the methods of production, and America grew to be an industrial power. Mass production made manufacturing quick and cheap.

Many important inventions of the Industrial Revolution were the work of Americans. Some examples are Eli Whitney's cotton gin and Elias Howe's sewing machine. Alexander Graham Bell invented the telephone, and Thomas A. Edison invented the phonograph and the electric light bulb. Farmers produced more food with machines. Many people left the farms to work in factories in big cities, and these cities became large markets for factory-made products. The federal government helped industry. It passed high tariffs (taxes) to keep out foreign products and supported the free exchange of goods among the states.

Work in pairs. Look only at this page. To answer your partner's questions, find the information and tell it to your partner. He or she will write the answers.

The Time of Reconstruction

The period of Reconstruction was from 1865 to 1877. During this time, Republicans of the North helped ex-slaves with housing, education, and food. Congress passed three Amendments to the U.S. Constitution:

- Amendment 13 put an end to slavery.
- Amendment 14 made all blacks citizens.
- Amendment 15 gave blacks the right to vote.

The North also wanted to punish the South, so Congress established military government in the southern states. Former southern leaders could not hold political office. Few white southerners believed that blacks were equal to whites, so they opposed the new laws. But black people had some political power in the South.

Although the differences between the North and the South were great, the United States became one nation again.

B **Now ask your partner these questions about the Industrial Revolution. Your partner will tell you the answers from the information on the previous page. Write them on the lines.**

1. What happened during the Industrial Revolution? _____

   _____

2. What did Eli Whitney invent? _____

3. What was Elias Howe's invention? _____

4. Who invented the telephone? _____

5. Who invented the phonograph and the light bulb? _____

6. Why did many people leave the farms? _____

7. What were the markets for factory-made products? _____

8. How did the federal government help industry? _____

   _____

C The Labor Movement

Since the Industrial Revolution, labor unions have fought for safe and healthy working conditions, fair wages, an eight-hour workday, job security, health benefits, pension plans, workers' rights, and civil rights.

Beginning Date	Union	Founder	Activities
1869	the Knights of Labor	Uriah S. Stephens	This union represented all workers, but it wasn't very successful.
1881	the American Federation of Labor (AFL)	Samuel Gompers	This union represented only skilled workers. It got them higher wages, shorter hours, and better working conditions.
1938	the Congress of Industrial Organizations (CIO)	John L. Lewis	This union represented semi-skilled and skilled workers. Its strikes shut down whole industries, not just individual factories.
1955	AFL-CIO	(merger)	The AFL joined the CIO and was powerful until President Reagan's government weakened the unions.

D Write the name of the union before each sentence: the Knights of Labor, the AFL, the CIO, or the AFL-CIO.

1. __CIO__ This union began with John L. Lewis.
2. _____ Uriah S. Stephens founded (established) this union.
3. _____ Samuel Gompers was the founder.
4. _____ This early union wasn't very successful.
5. _____ This union represented semi-skilled workers, and its strikes shut down whole industries.
6. _____ This union got higher wages, shorter hours, and better working conditions for skilled workers.
7. _____ This union was a merger of two big unions.
8. _____ President Reagan's government reduced the power of this union.

A Political Party and a Movement

Farmers formed the Populist Party in 1892. They felt that big business had too much power and that the system was unfair to farmers and industrial workers. They also believed in government control of the railroads and the telephone system. They wanted a graduated income tax (a higher percentage of tax on higher incomes), secret ballots (voting), and direct election of U.S. Senators by the people, not by state legislatures. Populists became mayors of towns, state representatives, and even Senators. They lost power after the election of 1896, but their ideas influenced the major political parties.

In the first part of the twentieth century, progressive thinkers formed a movement for social reform. Progressives believed in a "square deal" for ordinary Americans, so they tried to help workers, small businesses, and farmers. They wanted the federal government to control big business, take responsibility for the quality of food and drugs, and protect the environment. Some leaders of the Progressive Movement held political office and made reforms. Their ideas also led to several amendments to the Constitution: the Sixteenth Amendment established the federal income tax, and the Seventeenth Amendment allowed voters to elect U.S. Senators directly.

 Answer these questions about the political party and the movement.

	The Populist Party	The Progressive Movement
1. Who formed it?		
2. When?		
3. What did the members believe?		
4. What did they want?		
5. What did they do?		

Module 10G: The U.S. Becomes a World Power

A **Work in pairs. Look only at this page and ask your partner these questions about World War I. Your partner will tell you the answers from the next page. Take notes on the information.**

1. What happened to begin World War I?   *Heir to the throne of Austria-Hungary was shot. Austria-Hungary declared war on Serbia.*

2. What were the two sides in the war, and what European countries joined them?

3. Why did the United States enter the war in 1917?

4. Why was World War I called "the Great War"?

5. How and when did the war end?

6. What was the basis of the peace treaty to end the war?

7. What was the League of Nations, and why did it fail?

B **The Great Depression**

Because American goods were too expensive for other countries to buy and American wages were low, many investors lost confidence in the stock market and sold their stocks (shares, or part ownership, of companies). The Great Depression began with the stock market crash on Black Tuesday, October 29, 1929. Thousands of businesses, factories, and banks closed down, and millions of workers lost their jobs. This time of economic depression lasted for ten years.

President Franklin D. Roosevelt helped end the Great Depression with his "New Deal" of relief, recovery, and reform ("the Three R's"). His government relieved suffering with payments to unemployed people and loans to farmers and homeowners. It created government jobs to help the economy recover. Roosevelt also worked on economic reform to prevent future depressions.

Work in pairs. Look only at this page. To answer your partner's questions about World War I, find the information and tell it to your partner. He or she will take notes.

- It was Woodrow Wilson's plan for a world organization to prevent future wars. To avoid involvement in world affairs, the U.S. Senate rejected the Treaty of Versailles and the plan for the League of Nations.

- It was a "total war" because it involved the economies and the people of many countries. The U.S. Congress passed the Selective Service Acts to draft young men into the armed forces.

- The basis of the Treaty of Versailles was President Wilson's plan for peace, his Fourteen Points. Among other things, Wilson wanted freedom of the seas and trade and self-determination (the right of people to decide on their own form of government).

- Austria-Hungary declared war on the small country of Serbia because an assassin shot the heir to their throne.

- Americans were angry because Germany was using submarines to attack both warships and trade ships. They wanted to fight this "war to end all wars."

- The Central Powers were Austria-Hungary and Germany, and the Allied Powers were Russia, France, England, and Italy.

- Germany signed an armistice on November 11, 1918.

C   **Match the sentence parts. Write the letters on the lines.**

1. _d_ Many people lost confidence in the U.S. economy because...

2. ___ The Great Depression began because...

3. ___ Millions of workers lost their jobs because...

4. ___ The Depression ended ten years later because...

5. ___ The government made payments to the unemployed, farmers, and homeowners because...

6. ___ The New Deal government created jobs because...

a. businesses, factories, and banks closed.

b. Roosevelt wanted to relieve economic suffering.

c. investors sold their stocks, and the stock market crashed.

d. American goods were expensive, but wages were low.

e. President Roosevelt started the New Deal of relief, recovery, and reform.

f. it wanted the U.S. to recover from the Depression and prevent future ones.

Work in pairs. Look only at this page and ask your partner these questions about World War II. You partner will tell you the answers from the next page. Take notes on the information.

1. What happened to begin World War II?   *Germany invaded Poland.*
    Germany, Italy, Japan – the Axis. France, England, the Soviet Union –
    the Allies.

2. Why did the United States stay out of the war at first?

3. Why did the U.S. finally enter the war?

4. What happened during the war in Europe?

5. How and when did World War II end?

6. What were the effects of the war?

E Organizations and Plans

   After World War II, the Allied countries organized the United Nations (the U.N.) to solve problems among nations and keep the peace. Although this world organization had many of the same principles as the League of Nations, this time the United States was one of its original members. But at the same time the U.S. and the Soviet Union (the U.S.S.R.) were beginning to compete for power.

   In 1947 under the Truman Doctrine, the U.S. government gave $400 million in economic and military aid to keep Greece and Turkey free of Soviet control. Then the U.S. established the Marshall Plan to rebuild the countries of Western Europe, including its former enemies.

   The period of history after World War II is known as the Cold War because the U.S. and the U.S.S.R., with their opposing economic and political systems, have been trying to win influence and control over other countries through economic aid rather than weapons. In 1949 the U.S. and the nations of Western Europe formally allied in the North Atlantic Treaty Organization (NATO) to defend one another against attack. The U.S.S.R. began the Warsaw Pact with Eastern Europe in 1955.

Work in pairs. Look only at this page. To answer your partner's questions about World War II, find the information and tell it to your partner. He or she will take notes.

- President Truman made the decision to drop the atomic bomb on Hiroshima and Nagasaki. Japan surrendered on August 10, 1945.

- Germany invaded countries and enslaved, tortured, and killed many groups of people. The Soviet Union pushed back the attack of the German army. Italy surrendered in 1943. On "D-Day" in 1944, the U.S. General Dwight D. Eisenhower led the Allied armies to victory in Europe. In May 1945, Germany surrendered unconditionally.

- Congress wanted to avoid involvement in world affairs and stay neutral. In the 1930s it passed Neutrality Acts to keep the seas free.

- The army of Adolf Hitler invaded Poland. The other Axis countries (Italy and Japan) supported Germany, and the Allies (France, England and later the Soviet Union) opposed Germany.

- Over 22 million people died. The U.S. and the U.S.S.R. became the two leading powers in the world.

- Japan attacked Pearl Harbor in Hawaii, so the U.S. declared war on Japan, and Germany and Italy declared war on the U.S.

F   **Write T for true and F for false. Correct the false sentences.**

1. ___ The purpose of the United Nations is to solve world problems and prevent war.

2. ___ The U.S. Congress rejected the plan for the United Nations because it wanted to avoid involvement and stay neutral.

3. ___ After World War II, the U.S. and the countries of Western Europe began to compete for world political power.

4. ___ The Truman Doctrine is an example of the U.S. attempt to influence other countries through economic and military aid.

5. ___ Under the Marshall Plan, China gave aid to rebuild Japan.

6. ___ In general, the U.S. and its allies have a different political and economic system from that of the U.S.S.R. and its allies.

7. ___ During the Cold War, the nations of Western Europe have allied with the U.S.S.R. in NATO, and the U.S. has allied with Eastern Europe in the Warsaw Pact.

Module 10H: Modern Times

A **Work in groups of four. Each of you studies the information about a different aspect of modern times. In turn, summarize your information in your own words for the group.**

1. After World War II, America went to war twice against communist countries and their supporters. In 1950, North and South Korea could not agree on a common form of govermnent. North Korean communists, supported by the Chinese, invaded South Korea. The United Nations supported South Korea, and the United States sent troops (soldiers). With U.S. help, the South Koreans pushed the communist troops back to the thirty-eighth parallel.

Before the Vietnamese war, Vietnam was a colony of France. The people didn't want war, but they wanted freedom from foreign powers. Between 1961 and 1975, the United States intervened in the conflict on the side of the South Vietnamese anticommunists. The desire for independence gave the Vietnamese their fighting spirit. There were many protests against the war, and the United States finally withdrew.

2. The period of history since the invention of atomic bomb at the end of World War II is the Age of Technology and the Atomic Age. The world powers and people of all nations know that a nuclear war could destroy the whole planet. However, the superpowers, mainly the United States and the Soviet Union, continue to build missiles, bombs, military aircraft, and space weapons.

Fortunately, not all technology is designed for war. The United States sent its first satellite into space in 1958, and by 1969, the first American stepped onto the moon. Since then, the whole world has been using satellites and other space technology for communication, weather forecasting, science, and business. Both U.S. and Soviet shuttles are building space stations for both peaceful and military purposes.

At the heart of the Age of Technology is the computer. To school children, the computer is as important as the pencil. In the future, it can be used to improve human lives and to solve many of the world's serious problems, such as hunger and poverty.

3. In the 1950s, "the American dream" of wealth and freedom was easier for white males to achieve than for members of minority groups. Black Americans in the South, for example, could not attend white schools or live in white neighborhoods. Because of the policy of segregation, blacks sat in the backs of buses, used only restrooms for nonwhites, and ate at nonwhite lunch counters. In some southern states, black people could not even vote. Northerners, too, often discriminated against blacks, especially in jobs and housing.

In 1957, President Dwight D. Eisenhower sent U.S. troops to Little Rock, Arkansas, to force the all-white university there to accept black students. Between 1957 and 1970, as a result of the civil rights movement led by Martin Luther King, Jr., new laws helped blacks and other minorities to achieve equality. Presidents John F. Kennedy and Lyndon B. Johnson used King's ideas in their New Frontier and Great Society programs.

There have been great changes in the last forty years, but nonwhites have not yet achieved equal status today.

4. For a long time, American men did not believe in equality of the sexes. Women worked in low-level jobs and usually received lower pay than men for equal work. Few women finished college, and even fewer rose to executive-level positions with high salaries.

Today, American women are still fighting for equality because their salaries are generally lower than men's. However, many changes in the positions of the sexes have occurred. Half of all college students are women. More women are working than ever before, and their pay has risen, especially in government jobs, because it is easier for women to get jobs that used to be for men only. Many women own businesses, and others are executives in private business and government.

In recent years, many citizens have tried to add an amendment to the U.S. Constitution. The "Equal Rights Amendment" (ERA) states that both sexes have equal rights. But because many people fear that the amendment could take away some of women's special protections, such as the right to alimony (financial support after divorce) and exemption from the military draft, the amendment was not ratified (approved by enough states).

B   Match the sentence parts. Write the letters on the lines.

1. <u>d</u> North Korean and Chinese
        communists invaded South Korea
        because

2. ___ The United States finally
        withdrew from the Vietnam conflict
        because

3. ___ The United States and the
        Soviet Union continue to build
        missiles, bombs, and space weapons
        even though

4. ___ The whole world has been
        using space technology for
        communication, weather forecasting,
        and science since

5. ___ In the 1950s, black Americans
        could not attend white schools or
        live in white neighborhoods because

6. ___ Especially in jobs and
        salaries, nonwhites and women are
        still not equal to white males today
        even though

7. ___ Many American women are still
        fighting for equality today because

8. ___ The Equal Rights Amendment
        was not ratified because

a. great changes have
    occurred in the last
    forty years.

b. southern states
    followed a policy of
    segregation.

c. a nuclear war would
    destroy the whole planet.

d. the country could not
    agree on a common form of
    government.

e. many people oppose the
    loss of special
    protections for women.

f. women's salaries are
    generally lower than
    men's for equal work.

g. the people fought hard
    for the independence of
    their country from
    foreign powers.

h. the United States sent
    its first satellite into
    space in 1958.

C   Correct these false sentences.

1. After World War II, America went to war twice against capitalist countries and their supporters.

2. In the Korean War, North Koreans pushed Chinese troops back to the thirty-eighth parallel with help from the United States.

3. The Age of Technology began around the time of the discovery of the moon.

4. In 1957, President Eisenhower sent U.S. troops to Vietnam to oppose the followers of Martin Luther King, Jr. in the civil rights movement.

5. The New Frontier and Great Society programs were plans for U.S. and Soviet shuttle space stations.

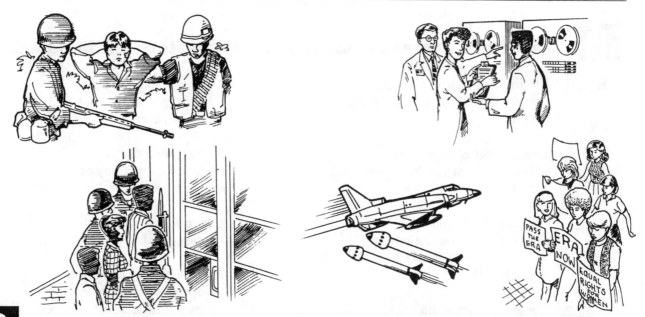

D **Do you support or oppose these statements about modern U.S. history? Work in small groups. Each student in turn chooses a different topic and speaks about it for one or two minutes. The other students tell their opinions and discuss the issue. Then summarize your discussion for the class.**

1. The United States should send troops to other countries if the conflict involves communism.
2. All nations have the right to be independent from foreign powers and to determine their own form of government.
3. The superpowers must continue to build missiles, bombs, military aircraft, and space weapons.
4. Because space weapons would destroy the earth, the United States and the Soviet Union should stop the development of space technology.
5. Because of the computer, humanity will solve many of the world's important problems, such as hunger and poverty.
6. Members of minority groups have not been able to achieve "the American dream" or equal status with whites because of the policies of segregation and discrimination.
7. The U.S. government has the responsibility of forcing the states to carry out civil rights laws and policies.
8. Men should do "men's work" and women should do "women's work" because the sexes are different.
9. Because there is no discrimination in job status and salary today, there is no need to fight for "equal pay for equal work."
10. The "Equal Rights Amendment" (ERA) is a necessary addition to the U.S. Constitution.

E **Make a statement of your own about modern U.S. history. Speak about it to the class for one or two minutes. The other students tell their opinions and discuss the issue.**

About Your State

Module 11A: Important State Events

A **Work in pairs. Look only at this page. For Items 1, 3, 5, and 7, ask your partner questions about California history and write the missing information on the lines. Begin each question with one of these words.**

who	what	where	when	why

For Items 2, 4, 6, and 8, answer your partner's questions.

EXAMPLES:　　Student 1: Where did the first white men arrive in California?
　　　　　　　Student 2: At San Diego Bay.
　　　　　　　Student 1: When did they arrive there?
　　　　　　　Student 2: On September 28, 1542.

1. On ___September 28, 1542___, the first white men arrived at
　　　　(date)
_____ in California. They met _____.
(place)　　　　　　　　　　　　　　　　　　　　　(people)

They were from _____, and _____ was their leader.
　　　　　　　　　(country)　　　　　　　　(person)

2. In 1769, Governor Portola came with a group of settlers from Mexico. He claimed the territory for Spain. Padre Junipero Serra built missions to teach Christianity to the native Indians.

3. On April 11, 1822, _____ raised the flag of
　　　　　　　　　　　　(person)

_____ over the Presidio (fort) at _____.
(country)　　　　　　　　　　　　　　　　　　(place)

4. In 1839, Captain John Sutter built the famous Sutter's Fort in the Sacramento Valley.

5. On July 7, 1846, _____ flew over the Customs House
　　　　　　　　　　(thing)

in Monterey. _____ claimed the territory of California.
　　　　　　　(country)

6. In 1846, James Marshall discovered gold at Coloma. Thousands of people hurried to California during the Gold Rush.

7. On May 10, 1869, railroad workers laid the last stretch of track to complete _____.
　　　　　　　　　　　　　　　　　　　　　　　　　　　　　　　　　　　　(thing)

8. In 1893, miners discovered oil in Los Angeles. In the following years, the population grew quickly because the oil industry brought the machine age to California.

A **Work in pairs. Look only at this page. For Items 1, 3, 5, and 7, answer your partner's questions about California history. For items 2, 4, 6, and 8, ask questions and write the missing information on the lines. Begin each question with one of these words.**

who	what	where	when	why

EXAMPLES: Student 1: Where did the first white men arrive in California?
               Student 2: At San Diego Bay
               Student 1: When did they arrive there?
               Student 2: On September 28, 1542.

1.   On September 28, 1542, the first white men arrived at San Diego Bay in California. They met the California Indians. They were from Spain, and Juan Cabrillo was their leader.

2.   In _____, _____ came with a group of settlers from Mexico.
        (year)   (person)

He claimed the territory for _____. Padre Junipero Serra built missions _____.
                         (country)   (reason)

3.   On April 11, 1822, Governor Pablo Sola raised the flag of Mexico over the Presidio (fort) at Monterey.

4.   In 1839, Captain John Sutter built _____ in _____.
                                  (thing)   (place)

5.   On July 7, 1846, the American flag flew over the Customs House in Monterey. The United States claimed the territory of California.

6.   In _____, James Marshall discovered _____ at Coloma.
        (year)   (thing)

Thousands of people hurried to California during _____.
                                     (period of time)

7.   On May 10, 1869, railroad workers laid the last stretch of track to complete the first transcontinental railroad.

8.   In 1893, miners discovered _____ in Los Angeles. In the following years,
                             (thing)

the population grew quickly _____.
                (reason)

B   Write the answers to these questions about California history.

1. Where did the first white men arrive in California?   San Diego Bay

2. Who did they meet there? _____

3. Where were they from? _____

4. Who was their leader? _____

5. What country did Governor Portola claim the territory of California for? _____

6. Why did Padre Junipero build missions? _____

7. What did Governor Pablo Sola do on April 11, 1822? _____

8. Who built Sutter's Fort? _____

9. Where did he build the fort? _____

10. What flag flew over the Customs House in Monterey, California in 1846? _____

11. What did the flag mean? _____

12. What did James Marshall discover at Coloma in 1848? _____

13. Why did thousands of people rush to California after that discovery? _____

14. What did railroad workers complete on May 10, 1869? _____

15. What did miners discover in 1893 in Los Angeles? _____

16. Why was this discovery important? _____

_____

Tell some important events of California history from these pictures and the words under them.

1.

1542 / the first white men
San Diego Bay
the California Indians
Spain / Juan Cabrillo

2.

1769 / Governor Portola
settlers / Mexico
claimed the territory / Spain
Padre Serra / missions

3.

1822 / Governor Pablo Sola
flag of Mexico
the Presidio / Monterey

4.

1839 / Captain John Sutter
Sutter's Fort
the Sacramento Valley

5.

1846 / the American flag
the Customs House / Monterey
the U.S. / the territory

6.

1846 / James Marshall
gold / Coloma
the Gold Rush

7.

1869 / railroad workers
the first transcontinental
railroad

8.

1893 / miners / oil
Los Angeles / population
the oil industry / the machine age

 If you live in a state other than California, find out the important events in the history of your state. Write them on the chalkboard and discuss them as a class.

Module 11B: State History

A **Look at the scenes from Los Angeles history and answer these questions about each one:**

1. What are the things in the picture and who are the people?
2. What do you think is happening?
3. What time of history do you think this is? Why?

1.

Spanish explorers

2.

mission life

3.

Mexican trade with Americans

4.

Russian trading posts

5.

the Bear Flag Republic

6.

the gold rush

7.

the Indian wars

8.

discrimination against the Chinese

9.

a population boom

10.

the motion picture industry

11.

life style of the automobile

12.

dams and aquaducts

B **Work in groups of four. Each of you studies the information about two different times in California history. In turn, summarize the information in your own words for the group.**

1.

The Spanish were the first white people to explore and settle in California. In 1540 Francisco Vasquez de Coronado set out from Mexico with a group of adventurers to explore California by land. Other Spanish explorers, such as Juan Rodriguez Cabrillo, came to the San Diego area by ship. Sir Francis Drake and his group of English explorers arrived at the northern California coast in 1579, but Spain was the only European nation to rule territory in California.

2.

For more than fifty years, Spain continued to control California with its chain of missions on the Pacific coast. The missionaries tried the teach the beliefs of Christianity to the native Indians. With the help of Indian workers, they grew fruit and raised cattle. Russian traders came from their settlements in Alaska to establish trading posts in northern California, but they never had much power.

3.

Mexico won its independence from Spain in 1821 and took over the territory of California. In the North, Canadian and American fur trappers and adventurers were exploring the Sierra Nevada Mountains. Mexican settlers were selling cattle hides and getting supplies from American traders. There were huge cattle, horse, and sheep ranches in the state, which the landowners ("rancheros") ruled like independent states.

4.

In the 1840s the U.S. government was pushing the nation's boundaries westward by encouraging Americans to settle in the Southwest and California. When a war started between the United States and Mexico in 1846, American settlers took over the Mexican military headquarters at Sonoma and proclaimed California an independent republic. This "Bear Flag Republic" lasted only a few weeks because the United States won the war and took California into the Union.

5.

The discovery of gold in 1848 made miners out of many California farmers, shopkeepers, and factory workers. The "gold rush" brought thousands of Americans from other states and immigrants from other countries. The "gold fever" of the "forty-niners" didn't last very long, but farming, manufacturing, trade, and other industries kept the new settlers in the state.

6.

In the 1850s, the U.S. government established a "reservation system" to keep the Indians out of the towns and cities. In the Indian wars between 1852 and 1867, Californians killed hundreds of Indians and forced others into the reservations. Discrimination and violence against the Chinese also began in the 1850s, and laws to limit immigration followed.

7.

Until about 1887, most of the residents of California lived in the northern part of the state. But interest in the health benefits of the southern California climate, advertising by the railroads, and the offers of real estate speculators (buyers and sellers of land to make quick profits) brought a population boom to the South. Southern California became famous for its orange orchards and other crops, but irrigation was necessary to bring water to the farms.

8.

By 1915, the motion picture (movie) industry was bringing income into California. It helped build the tourist trade and later brought the radio and television industries as well. The invention of the automobile and the discovery of oil greatly increased the pace of growth. Since that time, life styles in California have revolved around the automobile.

C Correct these false sentences.

1. The English were the first white people to explore, settle in, and control the territory of California.

2. Russia ruled California through a chain of trading posts on the Pacific coast.

3. While fur trappers were exploring the mountains in the South, Mexican settlers were trading supplies for cattle hides.

4. After the Mexican War, California never became a state of the Union because it was an independent republic.

5. The gold rush lasted a long time but brought few permanent settlers from other states or countries.

6. Native Indians and Chinese immigrants discriminated against American settlers and established reservations for them.

7. Until about 1887, most California residents lived in the South, but then there was a population boom in the North.

8. The movie industry, the invention of the automobile, and the discovery of oil have decreased the rate of population growth.

D Number these events from California history 1-9 in correct time order.

___ Spain established missions to teach Christianity to the Indians and to control California.

___ Spanish and English explorers, such as Coronado, Cabrillo, and Drake came to California by land and by ship.

___ California became a part of the United States and then a state of the Union.

___ Life styles in the state have revolved around the motion picture and television industry and the automobile.

___ Californians killed and forced Indians into reservations and discriminated against the Chinese.

___ American settlement in California increased, and settlers declared it the "Bear Flag Republic."

___ There was a population boom in southern California, the land of real estate speculation and irrigated farms and fruit orchards.

___ When Americans and immigrants rushed to California to find gold, the population increased.

___ The Mexican government took over California, but the "rancheros" ruled their ranches like independent states.

E Answer these questions about the history of California or your own state.

1. Who were the first Europeans in the area? When did they arrive?

2. Why did the early settlers come to the area? How did they live?

3. How did the area become a part of the United States and a state of the Union?

4. What important events or discoveries brought new settlers to the state?

5. Was there a population boom in any part of the state? If so, why?

6. What has brought people to the state in recent times, and why do they stay?

Module 11C: The State Today

A State Symbols

1. With a surprise attack in 1846, a small group of American settlers took over the village of Sonoma, Mexican military headquarters in northern California. They set up an independent republic. They designed a flag with a red star and a grizzly bear to represent strength and revolution. The flag said "California Republic" and gave their government the name "Bear Flag Republic." The government lasted only a few weeks because the U.S. Navy soon occupied Monterey, then capital of California, and declared it a part of the United States. But the Sonoma flag became the model for the California state flag that waves from all state buildings today.

2. In 1849, even before California became an official state of the Union, delegates met in Monterey to write a state constitution. They also adopted a design for a state seal. Today, the Great Seal of the State of California, which appears on state laws and other official documents, is not much different from that original design.

The state seal is a circle with the emblem of Minerva, the ancient Roman goddess of wisdom. According to legend, Minerva was an adult when she was born, so she became a symbol for a state that "grew up" very quickly. The grizzly bear from the state flag is at her feet. Wheat, grapes, a miner, and ships represent state industries. The word "Eureka" at the top means "I have found it" in Greek and is now the official state motto (phrase that expresses an important principle). There are thirty-one stars because California was the thirty-first state admitted to the Union.

3. In addition to a flag and a seal, each state in the United States has adopted plant, animal, and other symbols. The golden poppy is the official state flower of California, which has the nickname "the golden state." The redwood is the state tree, and the grizzly bear is the state animal. The quail became the state bird in 1931, after the Audubon Society called an election to choose an official bird emblem. California also has a state fish, the golden trout and a state mineral, gold. The state colors are gold and blue. Gold represents other state symbols, as well as the fruit of the orchards and the sunshine, and blue symbolizes truth, loyalty, and the waters of the Pacific Ocean.

B   **Match the phrases on the left with the words on the right. Write the letters on the lines.**

1. ___ the state flag

2. ___ the state seal

3. ___ symbol for a state that "grew up" quickly

4. ___ the state motto

5. ___ the state flower and tree

6. ___ the state animal, bird, and fish

7. ___ the state colors

a. an emblem on official documents that includes several state symbols

b. the golden poppy and the redwood

c. gold for orchards and sunshine and blue for the ocean and truth

d. the red star and grizzly bear of "the California Republic"

e. the emblem of Minerva

f. the grizzly bear, quail, and trout

g. "Eureka" ("I have found it.")

C   **In the boxes, draw the flag and seal of your state. Fill in the chart with other state symbols and their meanings.**

symbol	What is it?	What does it mean?
flag		
seal		
flower		
tree		
animal		
bird		
colors		
nickname		
motto		

Work in pairs. Look only at this page and read the following description of a trip through California. Your partner will work with the map on the next page.

1. We started our trip through California at Redwood National Park, on the coast near the northern border of the state. We camped out there among the tall redwood trees.

2. We took Highway 101 south and then State Highways 299 and 44 to Lassen Volcanic National Park. There were steaming streams, bubbling mudholes, and beautiful mountains and lakes there.

3. On the way south, we drove through "gold country" east of Sacramento. Some tourist attractions there are the place where the "gold rush" began in 1848 and the "ghost towns."

4. Then we took Interstate 80 to San Francisco, "the city by the bay." We loved the Golden Gate Bridge, the cable cars, the waterfront at Fisherman's Wharf, the museums, and the theaters. We walked up and down hills, through parks and squares, and through ethnic neighborhoods like Chinatown.

5. Next we took a trip inland to Yosemite National Park. We hiked through meadows and past huge sequoia trees to magnificent waterfalls.

6. Through the town of Merced, we returned to the Pacific Coast at Monterey Bay. The Monterey Peninsula, with Big Sur and the town of Carmel, is beautiful.

7. Our trip down Highway 1 and our tour of San Simeon, William Randolph Hearst's "castle on the hill," were fun.

8. We continued down the coast to Morro Bay and took Highways 41 and 198 to Sequoia National Park, with its giant trees. We saw Mt. Whitney, the second highest peak in the United States.

9. It wasn't far from there to Death Valley National Monument, with its dramatic desert scenery, ghost towns, and a mansion called Scotty's Castle. We stood at Badwater, the lowest point in the western hemisphere (282 feet below sea level).

10. Highway 127 and Interstate 15 took us to the Los Angeles area. In our week there, we took tours, visited tourist attractions, went shopping, and enjoyed the sunshine at the beach.

11. Finally we arrived in San Diego. We enjoyed Mission Bay Park, Sea World, Old Town, Balboa Park, and other tourist attractions.

12. We ended our tour of California at the southern border, which we crossed to spend a day in Tijuana, Mexico.

D **Work in pairs. Look only at this page and listen to your partner's decription of a trip through California. Ask questions if necessary. Draw a line on the map to show the tour route.**

 In small groups, plan a trip through your state. List the places you will visit and draw a line for your route on a state map. Then describe your trip to the class.

About Your Town or City

Module 12A: Important Local Events

A **Look at the scenes from Los Angeles history and answer these questions about each one:**

1. What are the things in the picture and who are the people?
2. What do you think is happening?
3. What time of history do you think this is? Why?

1.

prehistoric times

2.

California Indians

3.

mission life

4.

the home of "pobladores"

5.

trading with Americans

6.

"rancheros" and ranches

7.

fiesta time

8.

an orange orchard

9.

the growth of cities

10.

advertising

11.

the discovery of oil

12.

the movie capital of the world

B

Work in groups of six. Each of you studies the information about a different time in Los Angeles history. In turn, summarize the information in your own words for the group.

1.

The Los Angeles "basin" is a wide, round, low place among hills. Thousands of years ago, prehistoric animals such as the saber-toothed tiger, the giant ground sloth, and the imperial mammoth (elephant) came to the warm, wet climate of the basin. Their bones were found in the sticky tar of the La Brea Tar Pits. Today you can see the pits and models of the animals at Hancock Park (Park La Brea) on Wilshire Boulevard.

2.

The first people in the Los Angeles Basin were Indians. They lived in grass huts in villages, made clothing of animal skins and furs, and gathered seeds, nuts, berries, and plants for food. The men hunted wild animals and caught fish. The women made baskets. They cooked acorn meal (mush from the nuts of oak trees) in the baskets with hot stones and roasted meat over open fires. Today you can see model scenes of these Indian days at the Southwest Museum in Highland Park (near Pasadena).

3.

In 1771, a small group of Spanish missionaries began to build Mission San Gabriel in the Los Angeles Basin. Hundreds of Indians came to live near the mission and helped to build it with adobe bricks (clay, soil, and straw mixed with water). The missionaries brought in cattle and planted fruit trees. They made soap and candles from cattle fat. In later years, they built other missions, such as the San Fernando Mission and the San Juan Capistrano Mission. You can see these missions and others near the city of Los Angeles.

4.

In September, 1781, eleven families came from Mexico to begin a settlement in the Los Angeles Basin. They called the village "El Pueblo de Nuestra Senora la Reina de Los Angeles" (The Town of Our Lady, the Queen of the Angels). The "pobladores" (settlers) built houses of adobe bricks and furniture of wood and leather. They grew food, raised animals, and dug wells for water. Cattle was important to the pobladores. They ate the meat and sold the hides (skins).

Their lives were hard, but they celebrated birthdays, weddings, and other special occasions with big fiestas (parties). They dressed up, ate, sang, and danced. Today you can see some of their homes and buildings on the oldest street in Los Angeles, Olvera Street. In El Pueblo de Los Angeles State Historical Park, the street looks like a Mexican market place.

5.

In the early days, Spain owned Mexico, and California was a part of Mexico. The people of the Los Angeles Basin traded cattle hides for goods from Spanish ships. But after Mexico won its independence from Spain in 1821, they traded with Americans.

Without the support of the King of Spain, the missions had a hard time. The people of the area worshipped at the village churches, and cattle owners wanted to take the land around the missions where the Indians lived. When the Mexican government closed the missions in 1833, the land went to Spanish settlers and friends of the governor. Seventy large ranches were formed in the area, and the owners became "rancheros" (ranchers). They used the Indians as workers and became rich from the land and the sale of cattle and hides. But their good lives, with their many fiestas and bullfights, ended in the 1860s. Meat prices went down, there was a drought (long period of dry weather), and they had to sell their ranches at low prices.

6.

In 1846, American troops took over Los Angeles, and in 1850, California became a state of the union. Many people came to the area to buy land. Where there used to be ranches, now there were farms and orange orchards. Cities like Pasadena, Santa Ana, Santa Monica, Pomona, and others appeared almost overnight. Advertising for the mild climate, beautiful scenery, and beaches brought thousands of people from other parts of the United States. Land prices rose quickly. After the discovery of oil in the 1890s, the pace of growth increased. Los Angeles became the movie capital of the world. The weather, the ocean, the movie studios, and other tourist attractions still attract millions of visitors today.

C **Correct these false sentences.**

1. The Los Angeles area is in the shape of a spoon and fork.
2. The first people in the area were missionaries and "pobladores."
3. The missionaries brought in fish and wild animals, planted oak trees, and made baskets.
4. The first settlers from Mexico made homes from straw and furniture from bones.
5. In the early days, Mexico was a part of California, and California owned Spain.
6. After the missions closed, the land around them went to the Indians.
7. Between the 1830s and the 1860s, the "rancheros" had hard lives.
8. Land prices have never changed in the Los Angeles area.

Number these events from Los Angeles history 1-10 in correct time order.

___ The Spanish built missions, and the Indians lived near them.

___ The good lives of the rancheros ended when low meat prices and a drought made them sell their ranches at low prices.

___ Some families from Mexico began a settlement called "El Pueblo de Nuestra Senora la Reina de Los Angeles."

___ Indians in grass hut villages lived from food gathering, acorn meal, and the meat of wild animals.

___ People bought land, and farms, orange orchards, and cities grew quickly.

___ Mexico won its independence from Spain, and the residents of Los Angeles began to trade with Americans.

___ When the missions closed, friends of the governor became the "rancheros" of seventy large ranches in the area.

___ Advertising and the discovery of oil brought thousands of people from other parts of the United States.

___ Prehistoric animals came to the warm, wet climate of the basin.

___ California became a state of the union, and Los Angeles became an American city.

E **Match the phrases with the places to visit today. Write the letters on the lines.**

1. ___ prehistoric animals

2. ___ early Indian life

3. ___ mission life

4. ___ the life of the pobladores and the rancheros

a. San Gabriel, San Juan Capistrano, and other places

b. Olvera Street

c. the Southwest Museum

d. the La Brea Tar Pits

F **Answer these questions about the history of Los Angeles or your own town or city.**

1. What were the important periods of history?

2. How did the people live at those times? (What were their houses like, what did they wear and eat, how did they make their living, etc.).

3. Where can you see evidence of their way of life today?

Module 12B: Local History

A Look at the map and answer these questions:

1. What do you think the pictures show about local history? (What probably happened?)
2. About when did these events probably happen?

B **Work in groups of seven. Each of you studies the information about local history in a different place. In turn, summarize your information in your own words for the group. On the map on the previous page, show your classmates the place.**

1.

Cambridge, Massachusetts, is only a few miles from Boston, which the British held in the Revolutionary War. But Cambridge was a center of rebel activity. In 1775 soldiers marched from the town to the Battle of Bunker Hill. When George Washington arrived in Massachusetts to take command of the colonial troups, he lived and established military headquarters in a mansion in Cambridge. From this elegant house, he often rode to the hills around Boston to plan military strategy.

In the following century, this mansion was the home of another famous American: the poet Henry Wadsworth Longfellow.

2.

In 1763 French fur trader Pierre Laclede greeted Indians at the place that is now St. Louis, Missouri. French settlers began a town and trading post there the following year.

In 1817, when the Zebulon M. Pike landed in St. Louis after a six-week trip from Louisville, the steamboat era began on the Mississippi River. The Pike was the first of thousands of steam-powered boats with paddle wheels that changed St. Louis from a frontier town to the third largest city in the nation in 1870. But in 1874 the completion of the Eads Bridge, which joined Missouri to the state of Illinois, marked the end of the steamboat age.

3.

To make railroad construction easier, in 1854 the U.S. government opened Kansas to white settlers. The residents of the new territory were supposed to decide for themselves if Kansas should become a slave state or a free state. But when New England abolitionists began sending anti-slavery citizens to settle there, proslavery Missourians crossed the state border to vote illegally in territorial elections. Proslavery candidates won these elections, so their opponents formed their own local governments. In 1856 proslavery Southerners formed armed bands to destroy Lawrence, Kansas, the center of abolitionist power. John Brown led raids against slaveholders along the Kansas-Missouri border. During the Civil War William Clarke Quantrill, a young Northerner who believed in slavery, led a band of supporters in a raid of Lawrence, killing hundreds of civilians. The state became known as "Bleeding Kansas" in this violent period of history.

4.

After 1865 railroad companies in central California began to hire Chinese workers. The labor unions in San Francisco protested, but when the Central Pacific Railroad Company began to lay tracks in the Sierra Nevada Mountains, most white workers quit because the work was so hard and dangerous. The Chinese worked in groups of twelve to twenty men, each with its own cook and supervisor. Tea carriers brought hot tea to the workers, and the Chinese diet of rice, fish, and vegetables kept them in better health than the whites. But many of the workers died from accidents.

5.

The Navajo Indians began thinking of themselves as a tribe during the winter of 1863 and 1864. U.S. troops trapped several hundred Navajo families near Canyon de Chelly in northeastern Arizona. As punishment for stealing cattle, the soldiers killed the Indians' sheep, burned their corn, and cut down their fruit trees. Then they made the Navajo march three hundred miles to a camp at Bosque Redondo in eastern New Mexico. The Indians couldn't raise crops in the poor land there, and they missed their native home. Many of them died.

6.

Between 1889 and 1906 the U.S. government allowed white settlers to move into one part of Indian territory in Oklahoma after another. A signal gun started each stage of this famous "Land Rush." Thousands of settlers hurried into Oklahoma each day. In Guthrie, for example, at the end of the first day, there were settlers from 32 U.S. States, three U.S. territories, and six foreign countries. A land agent and a lawyer had already set up outdoor offices to settle land disputes. Most settlers were living in tents or their wagons, but they soon built wooden houses. After about a month, the town had a jail. Some of the prisoners were called "Sooners" because they had claimed land sooner than the law allowed. (Today Oklahoma has the nickname "the Sooner State.")

7.

The city of Chicago has been known for organized crime. At the beginning of the twentieth century, gambling was big business there. After 1919, when Prohibition made the sale of alcohol illegal, Chicago gangsters profited greatly from bootlegging (dealing in liquor illegally). By the early 1920s corrupt politicans were running the city, usually with the approval of the mayor, such as "Big Bill" Thompson. The famous Al Capone, "king of the Chicago underworld," didn't go to prison until 1931.

C   **Write T for true and F for false. Correct the false sentences.**

1. ___ For a time during the Revolutionary War, Cambridge, Massachusetts, was a center of rebel activity and colonial military headquarters.

2. ___ At different times General George Washington and poet Henry Wadsworth Longfellow lived in the same mansion.

3. ___ Spanish explorers started the settlement of St. Louis, Missouri, because they wanted to find gold there.

4. ___ When the Zebulon M. Pike landed in St. Louis in 1817, the age of the airplane began.

5. ___ When the U.S. government opened Kansas to white settlers in 1854, an era of peace began.

6. ___ The state became known as "bleeding Kansas" because supporters of slavery and abolitionists opposed one another in elections and violent attacks.

7. ___ In spite of union protests, only white workers could build the railroads in California in the 1860s.

8. ___ In the 1860s the U.S. government was treating the Navajo Indians of Arizona well because they were excellent farmers in the poor land.

9. ___ In the famous Oklahoma "Land Rush," the U.S. government took land from white settlers to give it back to the Indians.

10. ___ Oklahoma has the nickname "the Sooner State" because of the many settlers who claimed land before the government allowed them to.

11. ___ Gambling, bootlegging, and corruption in local government are examples of the organized crime that Chicago has been known for.

12. ___ Al Capone was a famous proslavery fighter who killed civilians in Lawrence, Kansas, during the Civil War.

    Turn back to page 85. Tell about local history from the pictures.

    Find out about one period of local history in your town or city. Make notes on the important facts and collect pictures. Summarize the information for the class and show the pictures.

Module 12C: The City Today

 A **Work in pairs. Look only at this page and read the following description of sightseeing in the Los Angeles area. Your partner will work with the map on the next page.**

1. We started our sightseeing tour at the Greater Los Angeles Visitors and Convention Bureau in the Arco Plaza downtown. We got free local maps, booklets, and lists of events in the city there.

2. First, we went to El Pueblo de Los Angeles State Historical Park. We saw the Plaza Church and the Avila Adobe, the oldest house in the city. We had a Mexican meal and bought souvenirs on Olvera Street. There was a fiesta in the "plaza" (the public square).

3. Second, we drove to Dodger Stadium. There was no baseball game there then, but we saw the "home" of L.A.'s major league baseball team.

4. North of downtown Los Angeles, we visited the Southwest Museum in Highland Park. There we saw scenes from early Indian life in the L.A. Basin.

5. Next, we took the Golden State Freeway (5) to Griffith Park. We toured the zoo, saw a nature museum, and watched a show at the Griffith Observatory.

6. The next day, we took the Ventura Freeway (101) and the Hollywood Freeway south to Universal Studios. We found out how movies are made and saw some entertaining shows.

7. Then we saw the landmarks of Hollywood on a bus tour. We enjoyed the footprints and signatures of movie stars in the sidewalk outside Mann's Chinese Theater and went to a concert at the Hollywood Bowl in the evening.

8. The following day, we saw the La Brea Tar Pits, with their models of prehistoric animals and exhibits, and the Page Museum in Hancock Park. The L.A. County Museum of Art is there on Wilshire Boulevard, too.

9. Then we toured Beverly Hills, with its shops, mansions, and elegant hotels.

10. Westwood was the next place we visited. We went shopping and took a tour of the campus of the University of California at Los Angeles (U.C.L.A.). We saw a dance performance in the theater.

11. The next morning was warm and sunny, so we spent it on the beach at Santa Monica. We had fun on the Santa Monica Pier and rode bicycles along Venice Beach.

A Work in pairs. Look only at this page and listen to your partner's description of sightseeing in the Los Angeles area. Ask questions if necessary. Draw a line on the map to show the sightseeing route and write the names of the places.

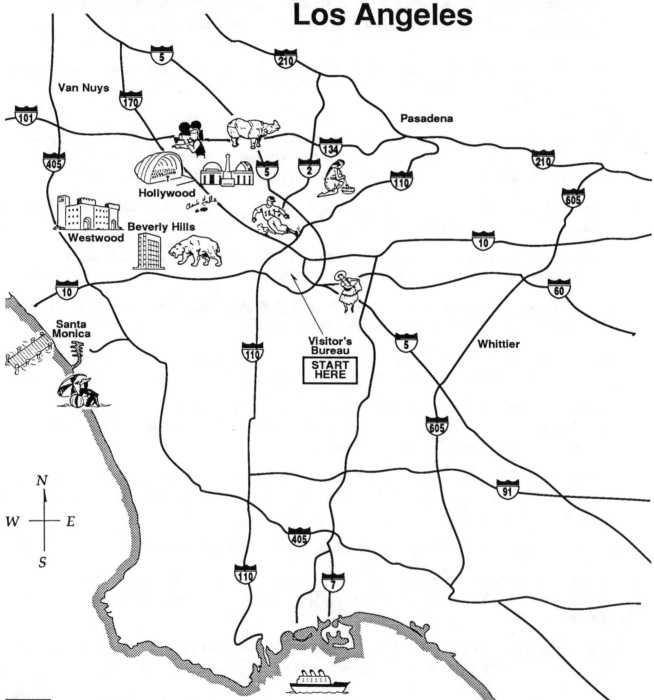

Los Angeles

B In pairs or small groups, use the map above or tourist booklets and maps of your city or area to plan a sightseeing tour. List the places to visit in order and tell the class the reasons for your choices.

C Getting Around the Area

The city of Los Angeles includes many communities, such as Hollywood, Westwood, and Boyle Heights, and Van Nuys and Woodland Hills in the San Fernando Valley. These are all sections of the city. But next to and even inside the boundaries of the city are over one hundred separate towns and cities, such as Beverly Hills, Santa Monica, Culver City, and Long Beach, each with a separate city government. And some areas of Los Angeles County do not belong to cities at all.

A large system of freeways connects the various parts of the L.A. Basin and the surrounding counties: Ventura, San Bernardino, Orange, and Riverside.

D Work in pairs. Look at the map on the next page to answer these questions:

1. What are some of the communities inside and the cities around Los Angeles?

   _____   _____   _____

   _____   _____   _____

2. What are the names and numbers of some of the freeways?

   _____   _____   _____

   _____   _____   _____

3. Name two communities or cities. What is the approximate distance between them? (Use the Scale of Miles.)

   from _____ to _____ = _____ miles

   from _____ to _____ = _____ miles

   from _____ to _____ = _____ miles

E If you live in a place other than the L.A. Basin, get a map of your town or city. Answer the questions in D and these questions about the area:

1. How is it different from the L.A. area (Examples: Is it smaller? Are there highways instead of freeways? Are all communities sections of the city itself?).

2. Which city is easier to get around in? Why?

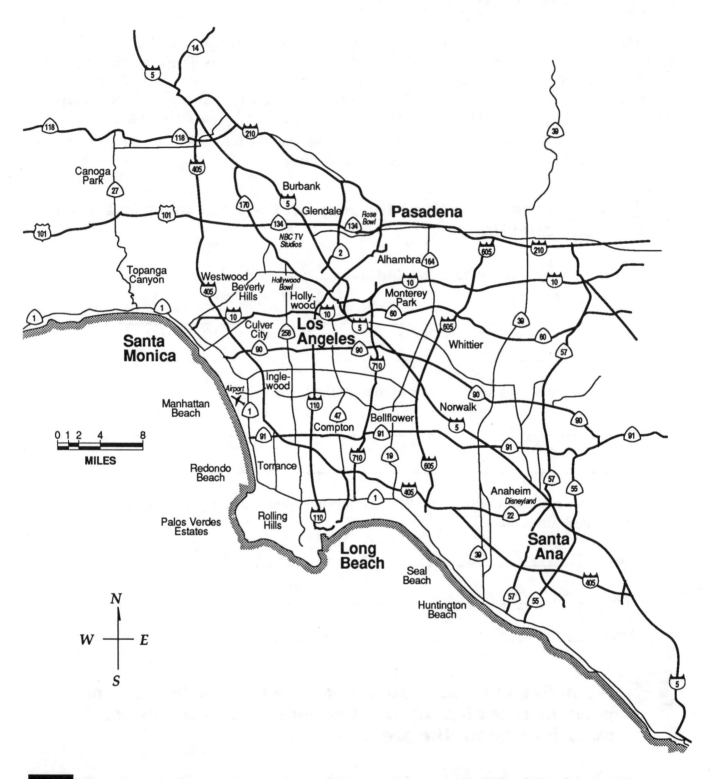

F Work in pairs. Ask and answer some questions of your own about the map above or the map of your city (Examples: How do you get from Santa Monica to Anaheim? Where is the L.A. International Airport?)